BOOK O

GOD DOESN'T DO EVIL
THAT GOOD MAY COME

The Truth About God Series

DELORES J. PORTER

Trilogy Christian Publishers
A Wholly Owned Subsidiary of Trinity Broadcasting Network
2442 Michelle Drive
Tustin, CA 92780
Copyright © 2024 by Delores J. Porter
Scripture quotations marked (KJV) taken from The Holy Bible, King James Version. Cambridge Edition: 1769.
Scripture quotations marked niv are taken from the Holy Bible, New International Version®, NIV®. Copyright © 1973, 1978, 1984, 2011 by Biblica, Inc.TM Used by permission of Zondervan. All rights reserved worldwide. www.zondervan.com. The "NIV" and "New International Version" are trademarks registered in the United States Patent and Trademark Office by Biblica, Inc.TM
Scripture quotations marked TCNT are taken from the Twentieth Century New Testament® (TCNT), Copyright © 1902
All rights reserved, including the right to reproduce this book or portions thereof in any form whatsoever.
For information, address Trilogy Christian Publishing
Rights Department, 2442 Michelle Drive, Tustin, CA 92780.
Trilogy Christian Publishing/ TBN and colophon are trademarks of Trinity Broadcasting Network.
For information about special discounts for bulk purchases, please contact Trilogy Christian Publishing.
Photo Credit: Cover photographer, Rebecca Webb Wilson
"Rainbow Waterfall," Iquazu Falls, Brazil
www.hawkeyenature.com
Trilogy Disclaimer: The views and content expressed in this book are those of the author and may not necessarily reflect the views and doctrine of Trilogy Christian Publishing or the Trinity Broadcasting Network.

10 9 8 7 6 5 4 3 2 1
Library of Congress Cataloging-in-Publication Data is available.
ISBN 979-8-89333-155-4
ISBN (ebook) 979-8-89333-156-1

DEDICATION

"I dedicate this book to all
who have ever had a loss of any kind.
It is written so you can learn the truth
that God is not guilty."

TABLE OF CONTENTS

Foreword 7

Introduction 11

Chapter 1: Who is in Control of Sickness,
Tragedy, and Death? 17

Chapter 2: Who is in Control if We Have Free Will? 37

Chapter 3: God Has No Pleasure in Death 51

Chapter 4: Where Did Death Come From? 59

Chapter 5: What is the Mosaic Law? 73

Chapter 6: What Really Happened in the Garden? 85

Chapter 7: What Caused Noah's Flood 101

Chapter 8: The Truth About God in the Book of Job . . . 109

Chapter 9: The Darkness is Unveiled 117

Chapter 10: The Rest of the Easter Story 129

Chapter 11: When Was the War in Heaven? 155

Chapter 12: Do Our Translations of the Bible Change
Scripture Meaning? 177

Chapter 13: Have We Caused People
to Run From God? 183

Chapter 14: Would the Real God Please Stand Up? 191

Charts 209

Notes 219

A Note from the Author 221

FOREWORD

God Doesn't Do Evil That Good May Come is the first of other volumes in which my friend and sister in the Lord, Delores Porter, will cover the subject; *Who is in control of sickness, death and tragedy*, and Where is God in the bad times? Delores brings to us a study of Scripture as it relates to the adversities of our daily lives from a layperson's point of view and with a passion to minister to the hurting people.

Her purpose of the study is to awaken in the hearts of people that Christ is the answer to all of the needs of mankind and to lead them to invest in the study of these things. This series of The Truth About God encompasses the study of God's Character and is to say the least a thought provoking study that will cause one to look deeper into the Scriptures provided in this study.

I have been pleased to read and study this volume and I cordially commend it to all Christians of faith, and to all who are interested in the Truth about God.

Dr. L. V. Rigney
Pathway Ministries

Jesus crying tears like rain from clouds
all over the Twin Towers on 9/11

This is the vision I saw while
praying on the morning of 9/12/2001.

What you are about to read in this memorial, which I call the Introduction to this book are words I felt inspired to write down the morning of September 12, 2001. With tears rolling down my face, a Kleenex in one hand and a pen in the other, these words were as clear as a nearly audible voice. I felt my heart would break with God's as He cried in pain and grief over what had just happened to America on September 11, 2001. This grief was doubled at the thought of the fables in the foundation our modern theology. God knew He would be blamed for such a horrible work of Satan; by His own His people and leaders of His Gospel, and that this could cause people to run from Him, instead of to Him.

INTRODUCTION

THE DAY AFTER THE DARKEST DAY IN AMERICA

A Letter from God
September 12, 2001

Dear America,

You are asking: How did this happen? Whose fault was it? Could it have been prevented? Why were America's churches filled last night on 9/11? Was it because they thought it was my wrath and judgment on America? Did they think they must go and repent of their sins lest I send some greater judgment?

Did they go pray out of their fear of Me? Were they pleading and begging Me for mercy to help the wounded?

It is through their prayers that angels are loosed, which enables heaven to move; then, at My commands, My angels help and minister to people.

Oh, my people perish for the lack of the knowledge of My Word and the knowledge of Me.

No, this is not my judgment on America. Do not believe that it took this horrible thing, at the cost of all these lives— this nightmare—to bring revival to America.

It only took One to come and die for the sins of this world!

It only took One to come and judge the prince of this world and give authority back to mankind to judge devils and break the power of darkness to bring real revival.

It took the sinless Lamb; I was that Lamb once and for all.

No one needs to give his or her life to bring revival.

I do not do evil that good may come! Without knowledge, man is confused; oh, so confused.

People will say, "Look what good came out of this! The churches are full!"

But I tell you, if they are coming with a confused mind because they think it was My wrath and judgment, this will not bring about a truly great and lasting revival to America.

It is My goodness and love that draws mankind unto repentance.

Without the truth of the knowledge of Me, America will perish.

Her enemy, Satan, will have more victory if Americans are told that I did this.

It is not I who brought this horrible disaster. Neither did I allow Satan to do it for My purpose. Believe Me; I had nothing—NOTHING—to do with it!

The spiritual temperature of the church in a nation affects the spiritual temperature of its nation.

The church has been cold and selfish, worried more about

their retirements and money than the harvest of souls.

If only every Christian in America really knew what the power of their prayers could do.

If they only knew My Word and that, after Calvary, I have given them each the weapons of warfare.

If they only knew that they wrestle not with flesh and blood, but the principalities of darkness, and that I will give them power over all the power of the enemy, there would never be a need to go to war with guns and iron.

If My people, any of them, had been deep enough in My Spirit, they could have heard My divine voice flow up out of their spirit to their mind (soul).

It is through My gifts that I communicate to My people the enemy's plans and warn them of what he is doing. I did it before; it is recorded in the Scriptures.

Some had heard in part, but it was so bizarre, they did nothing.

The Spirit of the Lord then reminded Me of these most precious promises from His Word:

I am the same yesterday, today, and forever. I change not; And My Word will not pass away.

Have faith in me, learn of me, for I will NEVER leave you nor forsake you.

Trust in Me; cast all your cares and worries upon Me because I care for you.

My yoke is easy and my burden is light.

Lean not on your own understanding, but learn of Me.

Receive My peace, for I have a peace like no other can give.

I am LOVE, and I love you with a greater love than you can comprehend.

I am Alpha and the Omega, the beginning and the end.

Sincerely,

Your heavenly Father, and Savior, Jesus

CHAPTER 1

WHO IS IN CONTROL OF SICKNESS, TRAGEDY, AND DEATH?

Since September 11, 2001, the world has speculated as to the true identity of those behind the attack on the World Trade Center. What happened that day rocked America to its core. But why do we say God allowed the attack to happen?

Why do we believe every bad thing that happens is either caused or allowed by God? Tsunamis, hurricanes, tornadoes—He's been blamed for them all! At the very least, He's credited with allowing pain, suffering, tragedy—even death—to permeate life. But I thought God was supposed to be a God of love! Doesn't He tell us to love others as ourselves, even to love our enemies? How do we figure a God of love could have a hand in any tragedy? Where has this idea come from? One day I was speaking with a nurse from St. Jude Children's Hospital. We were talking about what a God of love our God is. She shared with me that most of the parents at St. Jude are told by the counselors to accept anything that happens to their child as God's will.

They watch other children get better and go home while their child steadily grows worse and dies. It leaves them so depressed. Then they end up divorced or their lives become ruined by anti-depressants.

She agreed with me—cancer and death could not have come from a God of love. How has He been so misunderstood?

I imagine the sermons given across America the Sunday after 9/11 were the hardest ever brought to the pulpit. Many churches saw their largest turnout that day. Hearts were filled with grief and terror, and everyone was looking to their minister for help and encouragement. Still, it amazes me how two people can hear the same sermon yet garner entirely different things. To hear some of the sermons given that day, though, it's easy to see how people could become confused and disheartened.

A client from my hair salon told me, "My pastor said God didn't cause the terrorist attacks and quoted John 10:10, 'The thief cometh not, but for to steal, and to kill, and to destroy.' He said God gave us free will, so it was man who did this." However, another client of mine—who attended the same service—heard something entirely different: "My pastor said God was behind it. But why would God allow it? He could have stopped it. So in His wisdom He must have had a reason to allow it." She told me she'd taken an unsaved friend to church that day, one whom she'd finally convinced to join her. Afterward, her friend's response was, "Why would I want this?" She couldn't understand why she should submit her life to a God who was behind something so horrific. Why are so many turning away from God?

A client came into my hair salon for an appointment. She was sick that day, so I tried to encourage her by saying, "The Lord has healing for you."

"Well, it must just be His will for me to be dealing with this right now,"

she responded. "We can't expect to have perfectly healthy bodies . . . not down here at least."

This woman was a Christian, but she didn't seem to have any faith in the Lord's healing touch. She was allowing religious doctrine to steal her healing! And, sadly, this is the norm.

What are we missing here?

Each day, people across the globe experience great loss:

death of loved ones, illnesses that claim the lives of children, natural disasters. Even less life-threatening losses, such as being laid off or going through a foreclosure, can turn a person's world upside down. To claim that all these things are in God's will and purpose because He's in control only leaves people hurt and angry at God, it destroys their hope and leads them to depression, loss of faith, even suicide.

If someone asks, "Why did God take my loved one?" the answer always will be unsatisfying. But we need somewhere we can go to find the truth about death.

Why not go to God Himself?

The doctrine of a God in total control would say to those whose lives are devastated by natural disaster, "It's all in His plan." It would say to the parents of the child who has spent over half his life in the hospital, "God gave you a beautiful baby. Now He's going to take it away after allowing a long period of painful illness. Don't ask why. It's His will." To the sick it would say that if they don't get well, God must not want them to.

This cannot be right! In no way would God give illness when He went through so much pain and suffering to relieve and heal us from it!

Just the other day, I greeted a client by asking, "How are you and your family?"

She responded with, "Not so good. My daughter-in-law had a miscarriage. I guess God just wanted that one back."

My heart sank. "Oh, no!" I said. "It wasn't God. It was a sickness; a sickness of either the mother or the baby."

God has provided healing for all of us, even the unborn:

> *I call heaven and earth to record this day against you, that I have set before you life and death, blessing and cursing: therefore choose life, that both thou and thy seed may live.*
> **—Deuteronomy 30:19 KJV**

Some teach that God disciplines with illness, stress, and even death to get our attention so we will repent or learn a lesson. But God doesn't condemn or punish. In John 5:22 KJV, Jesus said, "The Father judgeth no man."

Can you imagine the hurt, confusion, and even condemnation the parents of the children at St. Jude are feeling? How can we tell them their child's illness is part of God's plan and purpose? Or, even worse, some sort of punishment for their past wrongs? How can we tell them God knows best and is sovereign and has His way in all things, yet this is what He has chosen for their child? I think we should be telling them it's God's will to heal sickness—not inflict it!

One of these young couples from St. Jude came to my salon late one night for the wife to get her hair cut and get away from the hospital for a while. Their two-year-old son was there for a brain tumor. He'd recently had surgery, but the doctor wasn't able to get the entire tumor. Soon after, his chemotherapy began. But these two were amazing. They had so much assurance and hope in the healing power of God. They were smiling and joyous in His promises.

The couple had a praying church family back home in

Kentucky, and welcomed prayer from anyone who would believe with them. They had the peace of God—divine assurance from the beginning that their baby would be fine and healthy.

And he was!

Their son has no cancer now, and they brought him in to see me when they came to town for checkups. They were filled with joy and later gave birth to their second child. Oh, if only this testimony could be duplicated over and over again! The death of any of these children is not the plan or the will of God.

The stripes on Jesus' back were for our healing!

There are those who believe every death is God's will.

I have often heard it said, "Well, it was their time to go." But I believe thousands have died prematurely because they didn't understand God's Word and the provisions it holds for their protection. There is a real need for the knowledge of how to pray the scriptures in faith through Jesus Christ as He intercedes and commands His angels to protect us and warn us of danger.

I remember having the opportunity to express God's love and goodness once when a young girl brought her mother in to get a makeover. She said, "I saw your picture in an ad and I told Mom, 'You need to go to her!' We're going out of town tonight to a big wedding and Mom needs help with her hair."

My new client sat for a consultation. We decided what to do with her hair, and I mixed color for her highlights. I had started on her weave when she began to share her past year with me.

"I look so awful," she said. "I haven't done anything to myself in about a year. I've gained a lot of weight; probably fifty pounds. My hair looks bad, my nails are bad, and I haven't put on makeup in so long." Tears filled her eyes as she opened her heart to me. "My husband was a truck driver. He was killed in a wreck driving his eighteen-wheeler. I just can't get over it. I still cry all the time.

"I just don't understand," she said. "I know God gave him to me. We had such a beautiful relationship. In my first marriage, I was abused. But this man was precious to me. I know he was a gift from God. He played the guitar and several other instruments. We sang together. I still keep his instruments in my closet."

She forced out her last words. "I don't understand why God took him away," she said. "I don't understand why it was his time to go."

I touched her gently on the shoulders. Her eyes were red and swollen. With confidence and assurance I said, "Oh, God didn't take him. And it wasn't his time to go."

"But He did! You see, when my husband topped this

hill and came around a curve, there was a wreck in the middle of the road. He ran his truck into an embankment to keep from hitting the people. There was nothing he could have done but wreck. I know God is in control, so He must have allowed it."

I could see hurt, anger, confusion, and depression had bound her. My heart cried. So, as I placed the foils in her hair, I shared the love and goodness of God. "God is a good God, and in Him is no darkness at all," I explained.

> *"This then is the message which we have heard of him, and declare unto you, that God is light, and in him is no darkness at all."*
> **—1 John 1:5 KJV**

"God is the giver of life," I told her.

> *"And the Lord God formed man of the dust of the ground, and breathed into his nostrils the breath of life; and man became a living soul."*
> **—Genesis 2:7 KJV**

We have been taught that God is in total control of life and death. This is simply not true. But where did death come from, if not from God? The Word says it is Satan who steals, kills, and destroys (John 10:10).

Satan is death's author. It was through Adam's sin that death then entered this world. It is God's will that we have life more abundantly, a life full of joy. It is His desire that we live a long life of health and prosperity. And what is this prosperity? It's living in His will, walking out His destiny for our lives, using the gifts and talents He gave us. This is when the joy of living comes to us.

It's God's will that we live to an old age. In fact, we are meant to live until our bodies just wear out and can't go any further! My husband's grandmother, Jewell Crisler (whom we affectionately call "Grandmother Jewell"), had a great outlook on life. Truly, she was an example of one who was blessed in the Lord. She lived to be nearly 105 years old. We had her 105th birthday party planned, but she wore out and had her party in heaven instead. She had outlived her eleven brothers and sisters and even some of her own children. She had a keen mind and was independent, caring for herself until the day she died. She had hip surgery when she was 100 years old but was walking again in no time.

When Grandmother Jewell was in the hospital for the surgery, she entertained the nurses with songs on her harmonica. She was truly a delight. Even nurses outside her unit would visit just to see "the 100-year-old woman." They'd ask her, "What do you contribute your long life of health to?"

She replied the same way each time: "Casting all my cares upon the Lord."

Grandmother Jewell knew the key to getting rid of stress

and holding on to a strong faith in God. She always had an encouraging word and testimony for those who took the time to listen. She was hardly ever sick. She exercised by doing the bicycle before she got out of bed every morning and touching her toes several times a day. She drank carrot juice. She was not sick when she passed away. She just raised both arms, looked surprised, lay back on the bed, and closed her eyes.

Scientists now say we could live to be 120 to 125 years old. "Then why do accidents like this happen to Christian people?" my client asked, referring to her husband.

I continued to talk as I checked her foils. "I believe Satan slips up on our blind side and pulls one on us, partly because of our lack of knowledge in the area of protection through prayer. Most people don't realize two-thirds of the angelic host goes to work protecting us when we pray; they are servants of the saved."

> *"Are they not all ministering spirits, sent forth to minister for them who shall be heirs of salvation?"*
>
> **—Hebrews 1:14 KJV**

(Note: A lexicon is the resource we use to study the meanings of the original words written in the Scriptures in their original language. Throughout this book, you will find King James Version *Strong's Lexicon* entries to help with our study. Please note that in each entry, what comes before the symbol ":–" is the definition of the original word and what comes after that symbol is every English word the original word was translated to in the King James Bible. The translated English words are printed in order of frequency, from most frequent to least frequent.)

Strong's Lexicon / minister / Greek #1248: diakonia dee- ak-on-ee'-ah from 1249; attendance (as a servant, etc.); figuratively (eleemosynary) aid, (official) service (especially of the Christian teacher, or technically of the diaconate):– (ad-) minister (-ing, -tration, -try), office, relief, service (-ing).

Strong's Lexicon / Greek #1249: diakonos dee-ak'-on- os probably from an obsolete diako (to run on errands; compare 1377); an attendant, i.e. (genitive case) a waiter (at table or in other menial duties); specially, a Christian teacher and pastor (technically, a deacon or deaconess):– deacon, minister, servant.

Many of us think angels just automatically protect us, that we are assigned a guardian angel to protect us until it's our time to die, then God simply tells them to step back.

There are thousands of books written about angels and most are pleasant to read. But many do not line up with the Word of God. I've chosen to trust God and His knowledge of angels instead of man's perception of them.

The Word says that angels were made to honor and obey the Word of the Lord. The Word of the Lord is in our mouths:

> *"But what saith it? The word is nigh thee, even in thy mouth, and in thy heart: that is, the word of faith, which we preach."*
>
> **—Romans 10:8 KJV**

It is through our prayers that Jesus commands His angels to run on errands for us:

> *"Bless the Lord, ye his angels, that excel in strength, that do his commandments, hearkening unto the voice of his word."*
>
> **—Psalm 103:20 KJV**

In Daniel's vision, the angel Michael came at his prayers:

> *"Then said he unto me, Fear not, Daniel: for from the first day that thou didst set thine heart to understand, and to chasten thyself before thy God, thy words were heard, and I am come for thy words. But the prince of the kingdom of Persia withstood me one and twenty days: but, lo, Michael, one of the chief princes, came to help me; and I remained there with the kings of Persia."*
>
> **—Daniel 10:12–13 KJV**

Strong's Lexicon / Michael / Hebrew #4317: Miyka'el me-kaw-ale' from 4310 and (the prefix derivative from) 3588 and 410; who (is) like God?; Mikael, the name of an archangel and of nine Israelites:–Michael.

I continued to teach my client: "Why would God ever want to lose any of His soldiers here on earth? It's through us that He moves and operates to win the lost harvest of souls!"

Jesus won victory and authority over the enemy (Satan) at Calvary, then He went to heaven. But not before promising to send the Holy Spirit to live in us and give us authority over all the power of the enemy. He said He would also be in us and that He and the Father are One. We have God joined to our spirit at salvation.

Jesus gave us the Great Commission right before He ascended into heaven. Now, it's up to us to pray according to God's Word in order to maintain authority over Satan and receive God's protection. The Bible says to give thanks in all things; so we are to start our prayers thanking God, giving Him glory:

Lord, I thank You for hearing my prayers, for loving me, and for commanding Your holy angels to be all around to protect me, keeping me alert and giving me wisdom to be safe. In Jesus' name, Amen

By the time my client's hair, manicure, pedicure, and makeup were finished, she was a brand new person—on the inside even more so than the outside! Not only did she look beautiful, she was glowing. I knew she was leaving full of a new hope and peace in a loving God, a God she now knew had not taken her husband away from her.

Later that day, she called me from the airport, her voice full of excitement: "Delores, I know God sent me to you today. I prayed that prayer you taught me, and I know angels were around to protect me. You aren't going to believe this, but we were getting ready to leave when the pilot said we were going to have to change planes. Apparently there was something wrong with the plane. Prayer works, it really works!"

This woman remained my client for a long time, but she wasn't the same person she was the first time she came in. She wore a smile every time I saw her. She had the peace and joy of the Lord, knowing He doesn't kill.

One of the most misused scriptures in the Bible is Romans 8:28 KJV, "All things work together for good to them that love God." It has been taken completely out of context and used to support the idea of an all-controlling God—the One who is in control over all things in our lives, good and bad. It was even used as part of a text on September 16th, the first Sunday after 9/11. It still amazes me anyone could say God was working the terrorist attack for our good! Verses 26–27 and 34 explain verse 28, but they are almost never mentioned along with verse 28:

> *Likewise the Spirit also helpeth our infirmities: for we know not what we should pray for as we ought: but the Spirit itself maketh intercession for us with groanings which*

> *cannot be uttered. And he that searcheth the hearts knoweth what is the mind of the Spirit, because he maketh intercession for the saints according to the will of God. And we know that all things work together for good to them that love God, to them who are the called according to his purpose . . . .It is Christ that died, yea rather, that is risen again, who is even at the right hand of God, who also maketh intercession for us.*
>
> **—Romans 8:26–28, 34 KJV**

What is being said here? All what things work together for good?

These verses are talking about all things in prayer working together: (1) our prayer; (2) the Holy Spirit praying for us and through us; (3) Jesus at the right hand of God, also making intercession for us. This is totally different than saying everything that happens—good or bad—happens for our good.

Romans chapter 8 essentially says that all things in prayer work together to help us get through this world's tribulations— to help us overcome them as more than conquerors in Jesus Christ. Do you see now what taking a scripture out of its context can do? It can change its entire meaning!

If God causes the tribulations of our lives in order to teach us lessons, He must also judge and condemn us in order to decide which distress to inflict.

Look with me at the first two verses of this same chapter:

> *"There is therefore now no condemnation to them which are in Christ Jesus, who walk not after the flesh, but after the Spirit. For the law of the Spirit of life in Christ Jesus hath made me free from the law of sin and death."*
> **—Romans 8:1–2 KJV**

Strong's Lexicon / condemnation / Greek #2631: katakrima kat-ak'-ree-mah from 2632; an adverse sentence (the verdict):–condemnation.

Strong's Lexicon / Greek #2632: katakrino kat-ak-ree'-no from 2596 and 2919; to judge against, i.e. sentence:– condemn, damn.

These verses make it clear: Jesus does not condemn us (judge against us) but instead protects us from the condemnation of the law of sin and death. I believe the misuse of Romans 8:28 is Satan's deception at work to steal the most powerful message available concerning prayer.

Doesn't it make sense to you that Satan would try to steal our knowledge of prayer, our most powerful weapon against him? Naturally, he wants us to blame God for everything he and our bad choices cause—even sickness and death—because he knows this will turn people away from God. This will become clearer in the next few chapters.

The last few verses in Romans chapter 8 are some of the most comforting verses in the Bible:

> *"Who shall separate us from the love of Christ? shall tribulation, or distress, or persecution, or famine, or nakedness, or peril, or sword? . . . Nay, in all these things we are more than conquerors through him that loved us. For I am persuaded, that neither death, nor life, nor angels, nor principalities, nor powers, nor things present, nor things to come, Nor height, nor depth, nor any other creature, shall be able to separate us from the love of God, which is in Christ Jesus our Lord."*
>
> **—Romans 8:35, 37–39 KJV**

God is for us and nothing or no one can separate us from His bountiful love. But the knowledge of God is the key. The more of it we have, the less Satan can deceive us.

> *"My people are destroyed for lack of knowledge: because thou hast rejected knowledge."*
>
> **—Hosea 4:6 KJV**

> *"Whom shall he teach knowledge? And whom shall he make to understand doctrine? them that are weaned from the milk . . . For precept must be upon precept, precept upon precept; line upon line, line upon line; here a little, and there a little."*
>
> **—Isaiah 28:9–10 KJV**

Most Christians haven't studied the Bible enough to be weaned from the milk of the Word—its simple foundational truths. Like spiritual infants, we are not yet ready to digest the meat of the Word. But if we pray and study, the Spirit of God (the Holy Spirit) will teach us the knowledge of His character and give us insight into His Word.

And we will gain understanding, precept upon precept and line upon line:

> *"But the Comforter, which is the Holy Ghost, whom the Father will send in my name, he shall teach you all things, and bring all things to your remembrance, whatsoever I have said unto you."*
>
> **—John 14:26 KJV**

I heard a recording shortly after 9/11 of one of the most popular Bible teachers reading Romans 8:28 from a modern translation: The Twentieth Century New Testament. The version had completely changed the verse's meaning. His translation read, "God causes all things to work together for the good." What's worse, he was preaching this sermon in New York, telling everyone that God is in total control, that He either causes or allows everything to happen. He said, "God is a God of judgment and condemnation." But the Word plainly says:

> *"For the Father judgeth no man, but hath committed all judgment unto the Son."*
>
> **—John 5:22 KJV**

Keep in mind, Jesus did come here to judge, but He came to judge the prince of this earth—not man.

Look at the word "judgeth" or krino in Greek:

Strong's Lexicon / judgeth / Greek #2919: krino kree'- know properly, to distinguish, i.e. decide (mentally or judicially); by implication, to try, condemn, punish:–avenge, conclude, condemn, damn, decree, determine, esteem, judge, go to (sue at the) law, ordain, call in question, sentence to, think.

Using a lexicon to find the true meaning of the original word, you can see clearly that God doesn't judge, condemn, or punish. There you have scriptural proof that God is not in charge of death. He did not create death and He has absolutely no pleasure in it.

I don't intend to point fingers at those who believe God causes or allows everything. And I don't want to judge those who teach it. They simply can't get past the doctrine of an all-controlling God. Ministers are taught this theory starting all the way back in Bible school—even farther back if they grew up in the church. When something is that deeply instilled, it can be hard for a person to get around. For this reason, this book will use scripture to confirm everything it asserts about who God really is. As you read through these pages, you will get to know God . . . in His own Words.

CHAPTER 2
WHO IS IN CONTROL IF WE HAVE FREE WILL?

Modern theology seems to have a hard time answering this question. Yet it remains of vast importance to our understanding of God. I believe the same Holy Spirit that moved upon the men of old, anointing them to write down the Word of God, can also reveal to us the truth of this and other haunting questions:

> *But the Comforter, which is the Holy Ghost, whom the Father will send in my name, he shall teach you all things, and bring all things to your remembrance, whatsoever I have said unto you.*
>
> **—John 14:26 KJV**

> *But the anointing which ye have received of him abideth in you, and ye need not that any man teach you: but as the same anointing teacheth you of all things, and is truth, and is no lie, and even as it hath taught you, ye shall abide in him.*

—1 John 2:27 KJV

Both angels and mankind were given free will by God's covenant (law or word). In fact, free will and sowing and reaping are as much a part of God's character as is His very substance: love.

People can be made to do a lot of things, but no one can make someone else love them. God's intention was to sow (give) love to the angels and mankind and to reap (receive) their love, fellowship, and communion in return. God's law of sowing and reaping love is called the law of the Spirit of life. (See charts 1 and 3.) When God sowed love to the angels, they sowed love back.

But God loved first:

> *We love him, because he first loved us.*
> —1 John 4:19 KJV

> *He that loveth not knoweth not God; for God is love. In this was manifested the love of God toward us, because that God sent his only begotten Son into the world, that we might live through him. Herein is love, not that we loved God, but that he loved us, and sent his Son to be the propitiation for our sins.*
> —1 John 4:8-10 KJV

God gave us the freedom to love Him or not to love Him. The choice was and is ours. That is free will. But because of free will, God can't save us from the law of sin and death—at least not by Himself—because there is free will in the word whosoever:

> *For with the heart man believeth unto righteousness; and with the mouth confession is made unto salvation. For the scripture saith, Whosoever believeth on him shall not be ashamed. For there is no difference between the Jew and the Greek: for the same Lord over all is rich unto all that call upon him. For whosoever shall call upon the name of the Lord shall be saved.*
>
> **—Romans 10:10–13 KJV**

But where did the law of sin and death come from? Out of the law of sowing and reaping, Satan's sin "created" the law of sin and death. God's Word cannot change; just as love reaped love, sin had to reap judgment and death.

But judgment and death were never God's idea. (See charts 4 and 5.)

Satan was created perfect in all his ways, and he remained so until sin, pride, rebellion, jealousy, and envy were found in him:

> *Thou art the anointed cherub that covereth; and I have set thee so: thou wast upon the holy mountain of God; thou hast walked up and down in the midst of the stones of fire. Thou wast perfect in thy ways from the day*

> *that thou wast created, till iniquity was found in thee.*
>
> **—Ezekiel 28:14–15 KJV**

Jesus tells us that Satan was the first liar, the father or beginner of lies:

> *Ye are of your father the devil, and the lusts of your father ye will do. He was a murderer from the beginning, and abode not in the truth, because there is no truth in him. When he speaketh a lie, he speaketh of his own: for he is a liar, and the father of it.*
>
> **—John 8:44 KJV**

Jesus came to redeem us from the curse of this law. The following two verses are some of the key scriptures in this book:

> *There is therefore now no condemnation to them which are in Christ Jesus, who walk not after the flesh, but after the Spirit. For the law of the Spirit of life in Christ Jesus hath made me free from the law of sin and death.*
>
> **—Romans 8:1–2 KJV**

According to the Scriptures, we are each in control of our own choices. We have been so blinded to believe God is in control of every event on earth. God gave the earth to the sons of men:

> *The heaven, even the heavens, are the Lord's:*

> but the earth hath he given to the children of men.
>
> **—Psalm 115:16 KJV**

> Know ye not, that to whom ye yield yourselves servants to obey, his servants ye are to whom ye obey; whether of sin unto death, or of obedience unto righteousness?
>
> **—Romans 6:16 KJV**

God is love.

> He that loveth not knoweth not God; for God is love.
>
> **—1 John 4:8 KJV**

And love thinks no evil.

> Charity [love] suffereth long, and is kind; charity envieth not; charity vaunteth not itself, is not puffed up, Doth not behave itself unseemly, seeketh not her own, is not easily provoked, thinketh no evil.
>
> **—1 Corinthians 13:4–5 KJV**

Every time the word charity is used in the Bible, it's actually the Greek word agape, meaning godly love:

Strong's Lexicon / charity / Greek #26: agape ag-ah'-pay from 25; love, i.e. affection or benevolence; specially (plural) a love-feast:–(feast of) charity(-ably), dear, love.

This tells us sin and rebellion were not even in God's thoughts. Sin was nonexistent until Satan sinned. Sin is not a created substance but is the absence of love. It is an act of rebellion based on free will. Because God cannot go back on His Word, He couldn't change His law of sowing and reaping simply because Satan perverted it!

Free will and sowing and reaping were meant to be selfless gifts from God. Have you noticed Satan still tries to pervert the things God created to be the most beautiful? Sex, for instance, was created by God to be an innocent gift to Adam and Eve. It was meant to create a oneness and a physical way for them to show each other love and to create a child through that love.

Here is an analogy or parable my brother-in-law came up with. It explains how Satan perverted or poisoned God's beautiful law meant for the sowing and reaping of love:

Betty made a delicious pie and sent it to her neighbor as a gift of love. But when Betty's neighbor ate it, she died. Oh, what a story! The whole town blamed Betty for killing her neighbor! And it may have looked like that to those who didn't understand and know that an evil one got to it and poisoned it before it could reach her neighbor's house.

Just like the pie, God's beautiful law of sowing and reaping was poisoned by Satan. God intended for His covenant with the angels to operate in and through agape, or love. This is the law of the Spirit of life.

Remember, God's Word can never be altered, and He esteems His Word higher than His name:

> *My covenant will I not break, nor alter the thing that is gone out of my lips.*
>
> **—Psalm 89:34 KJV**

> *Be not deceived; God is not mocked: for whatsoever a man soweth, that shall he also reap. For he that soweth to his flesh shall of the flesh reap corruption; but he that soweth to the Spirit shall of the Spirit reap life everlasting.*
>
> **—Galatians 6:7–8 KJV**

(See chart 1.)

Keep in mind, Jesus was God's Word in heaven before He came to earth in a human body:

> *In the beginning was the Word, and the Word was with God, and the Word was God . . . And the Word was made flesh, and dwelt among us, (and we beheld his glory, the glory as of the only begotten of the Father,) full of grace and truth.*
>
> **—John 1:1, 14 KJV**

God put Adam and Eve in charge, to subdue and have dominion over all the earth:

> *And God blessed them, and God said unto them, Be fruitful, and multiply, and replenish*

> *the earth, and subdue it: and have dominion over the fish of the sea, and over the fowl of the air, and over every living thing that moveth upon the earth.*
>
> **—Genesis 1:28 KJV**

Strong's Lexicon / subdue / Hebrew #3533: kabash kaw-bash' a primitive root; to tread down; hence, negatively, to disregard; positively, to conquer, subjugate, violate:– bring into bondage, force, keep under, subdue, bring into subjection.

Who were Adam and Eve to subdue? It had to be Satan and his fallen angels. It could not have been the animals because they were all harmless. At that time, man and animals were vegetarian and did not kill for food. But Adam and Eve's sin put the whole earth and its inhabitants under the curse of the law of sin and death, bringing man lower than the angels. When they sinned, they gave over to Satan the dominion over the earth God had given them, thus making Satan its prince. What God had given man, man gave to Satan.

Natural disasters, which kill and destroy, come from evil, the curse that came from perverting the law of sowing and reaping.

They do not come from God. God is not guilty. God made the earth so perfect it didn't even have to rain. The ground was watered from beneath. Like a giant terrarium, a mist came up and kept every plant watered. What a garden

Eden must have been! Can you imagine walking in such a place, covered with perfect organic plants and beautiful flowers offering every pleasing scent imaginable? I think we will see this same perfection in the new heaven and earth.

I believe our failure to understand the law of sowing and reaping and the role it has played is the reason God is blamed for all things, both good and evil. The law of sin and death is mentioned throughout the New Testament, but these days it's hardly ever taught. Most scholars teach that it and the Mosaic Law are one and the same. But when we understand their differences, it's easy to know which law a particular scripture is talking about. The churches that received the letters of the New Testament must have also known the difference, because often when Paul or the other authors talked about these laws, they didn't name the law, they'd only describe it by its features.

Since, as Jesus said, the Father (in His deity) judges no man, God had to become man in order to judge Satan and win back mankind to Himself; that gave back to us what Adam lost: perfect communion with God and the ability to live under the protection of the law of the Spirit of life.

> *For since by man [Adam] came death, by man [Jesus] came also the resurrection of the dead. For as in Adam all die, even so in Christ shall all be made alive.*
>
> **—1 Corinthians 15:21–22 KJV**

Before Jesus went to the cross, He said:

> *Now is the judgment of this world: now shall the prince of this world be cast out. And I, if I be lifted up from the earth, will draw all men unto me.*
>
> **—John 12:31–32 KJV**

Jesus did win that victory over Satan at Calvary. If we use our free will to choose salvation, we are once again made higher than the angels and given back dominion—power over evil:

> *Know ye not that we shall judge angels? how much more things that pertain to this life?*
>
> **—1 Corinthians 6:3 KJV**

> *Behold, I give unto you power to tread on serpents and scorpions, and over all the power of the enemy: and nothing shall by any means hurt you.*
>
> **—Luke 10:19 KJV**

As we established in chapter 1, it is at our prayers that Jesus commands His angels to run errands for us, becoming ministering spirits to serve and assist us. They will also assist us as we pray deliverance to set people free from the bondage of evil spirits. Through the power of God's Word and the prayers of faith, God has given back to us power over our enemies: Satan and his demonic fallen angels. My passion for writing this book has come with my concern and realization that we, the Christian body of Christ, have not been taking up our responsibility to subdue evil.

> *Submit yourselves therefore to God. Resist the devil, and he will flee from you.*
>
> **—James 4:7 KJV**

Jesus said He would send the Comforter, the Holy Spirit, to live in us; through us He will reprove the world of sin, of righteousness, and of judgment:

> *Nevertheless I tell you the truth; It is expedient for you that I go away: for if I go not away, the Comforter will not come unto you; but if I depart, I will send him unto you. And when he is come, he will reprove the world of sin, and of righteousness, and of judgment . . . Of judgement, because the prince of this world is judged.*
>
> **—John 16:7–8, 11 KJV**

We are to judge evil, not people.

> *But this man [Jesus], after he had offered one sacrifice for sins for ever, sat down on the right hand of God; From henceforth expecting [waiting] till his enemies [Satan and his demonic spirits] be made his footstool.*
>
> **—Hebrews 10:12–13 KJV**

Who could make God's enemies His footstool? We have been given this power by Christ!

> *Behold, I give unto you power to tread on serpents and scorpions, and over all the power of the enemy: and nothing shall by any means hurt you.*
>
> **—Luke 10:19 KJV**

If Jesus is sitting at the right hand of God waiting until His enemies are made His footstool, could we be prolonging the wait for Christ's next big event, His Second Coming to earth?

Let us look at Jesus' words to us before He ascended to heaven. As you can see, He gave us the charge to do His work on earth, to build the kingdom of God, to bring souls back to Him.

> *And Jesus came and spake unto them, saying, All power is given unto me in heaven and in earth.*
>
> **—Matthew 28:18 KJV**

He has given that power and charge here on earth back to mankind, to all who will believe. He is saying to you:

> *Go ye therefore, and teach all nations, baptizing them in the name of the Father, and of the Son, and of the Holy Ghost: teaching them to observe all things whatsoever I have commanded you: and, lo, I am with you*

always, even unto the end of the world. Amen.
   —Matthew 28:19–20 KJV

While God is not in control of us nor this world and its tribulations, we can understand from these scriptures that Jesus' victory at Calvary did a lot more than most have realized. By our free will we can receive Christ as Savior, be empowered by the Holy Spirit, join God's army, subdue evil, and win back the lost to God through Christ. This is our part of God's plan, Divine Partnership. (We will have more about God's Divine Partnership throughout my books; it seems to have been left out of our modern teaching.)

CHAPTER 3
GOD HAS NO PLEASURE IN DEATH

And as it is appointed unto men once to die, but after this the judgment.

—Hebrews 9:27 KJV

Who appointed us to die? It wasn't God. God never had anything to do with death. He has no pleasure in death:

For I have no pleasure in the death of him that dieth, saith the Lord God: wherefore turn yourselves, and live ye.

—Ezekiel 18:32 KJV

Say unto them, As I live, saith the Lord God, I have no pleasure in the death of the wicked; but that the wicked turn from his way and live: turn ye, turn ye from your evil ways; for why will ye die, O house of Israel?

—Ezekiel 33:11 KJV

The dead can never praise Him on this earth for His mighty works in their lives. They can no longer bear witness for His goodness or draw people to Him:

> *The dead praise not the Lord, neither any that go down into silence.*
>
> **—Psalm 115:17 KJV**

God is not the destroyer of the body but the Savior of it. It is Satan who steals, kills, and destroys:

> *The thief cometh not, but for to steal, and to kill, and to destroy: I am come that they might have life, and that they might have it more abundantly. I am the good shepherd: the good shepherd giveth his life for the sheep.*
>
> **—John 10:10–11 KJV**

So who did appoint us to death? Adam and Eve appointed all mankind to the "first death" or physical death. God never sentenced us to die! Jesus is the giver of life. He gave His life so we could live forever:

> *For since by man [Adam] came death, by man [Jesus Christ] came also the resurrection of the dead. For as in Adam all die, even so in Christ shall all be made alive.*
>
> **—1 Corinthians 15:21–22 KJV**

As we studied in chapter 2, God's everlasting covenants with the angels and mankind are free will and sowing and reaping. (See Chart #1 and Chart #2.) He cannot interfere with or go against our free will. He cannot stop the actions of man upon this earth and the evils that they sow; if He could, there would be no murder, no human slavery, no rape, no terrorist acts. Remember, He gave the earth to man:

> *Ye are blessed of the Lord which made heaven and earth. The heaven, even the heavens, are the Lord's: but the earth hath he given to the children of men.*
> **—Psalm 115:15–16 KJV**

Adam and Eve may have sentenced us to the "first death," *the physical death,* but we appoint ourselves to the "second death" by refusing our salvation through Jesus, paid for at Calvary. To be eternally separated from the magnificent presence of God is called the "second death."

> *He that hath an ear, let him hear what the Spirit saith unto the churches; he that overcometh shall not be hurt of the second death.*
> **—Revelation 2:11 KJV**

God always tells us to turn from our wicked ways and choose life. Our ability to choose either life or death demonstrates our free will.

But one day there will be no death.

> *The last enemy that shall be destroyed is death.*
> **—1 Corinthians 15:26 KJV**

Strong's Lexicon / enemy / Greek #2190: echthros echthros' from a primary echtho (to hate); hateful (passively, odious, or actively, hostile); usually as a noun, an adversary (especially Satan):–enemy, foe.

And the enemy (Satan) will be cast into the lake of fire and tormented forever. This is why he tries to deceive the church: to hinder God's last day revival and prolong his reign on earth.

> *And the devil that deceived them was cast into the lake of fire and brimstone, where the beast and the false prophet are, and shall be tormented day and night for ever and ever.*
> **—Revelation 20:10 KJV**

If God has no pleasure or part in death, what is meant by Psalm 116?

> *Precious in the sight of the Lord is the death of his saints.*
> **—Psalm 116:15 KJV**

This verse can seem confusing and contradictory, until a study of the word precious is done:

Strong's Lexicon / precious / Hebrew #3368: yaqar yaw-kawr' from 3365; valuable (obj. or subj.):–brightness, clear, costly, excellent, fat, honourable women, precious, reputation.

It's clear to me that the author is trying to express that it is costly to God to lose one of His soldiers on earth. He or she can no longer witness of God's goodness or lead another soul to Christ. That's a huge loss to God's kingdom! Every person is needed and is valuable to the body of Christ to do His work: winning the lost and ministering to one another:

> *For by one Spirit are we all baptized into one body, whether we be Jews or Gentiles, whether we be bond or free; and have been all made to drink into one Spirit. For the body is not one member, but many . . . And the eye cannot say unto the hand, I have no need of thee: nor again the head to the feet, I have no need of you.*
> **—1 Corinthians 12:13–14, 21 KJV**

Paul writes in Philippians that "to die is gain." At first glance, this sounds like he was saying it is profitable for man to die:

> *For to me to live is Christ, and to die is gain. But if I live in the flesh, this is the fruit of my labour: yet what I shall choose I wot not.*
> **—Philippians 1:21–22 KJV**

But to understand this passage better, one must consider the context in which it was written. Paul was writing from prison. In his physical condition, he would have craved death over living with hands and feet tied; heaven would have sounded good to him. Yet he was writing to the church in Philippi telling them, "It would be more profitable for them for him to get out of prison so he could come back and minister to them." Paul had faith that he would get out of prison and minister again.

Then Paul said:

> *Nevertheless to abide in the flesh is more needful for you. And having this confidence, I know that I shall abide and continue with you all for your furtherance and joy of faith; That your rejoicing may be more abundant in Jesus Christ for me by my coming to you again.*
>
> **—Philippians 1:24–26 KJV**

The following poem was written by Douglas Malloch (printed in *Christ the Healer,* copyright 1973). I believe Malluch was inspired by the Holy Spirit in illumination of Scripture that many leaders today have not seen.

BLAME NOT GOD

Death comes, and then we blame our God,
And weakly say, "Thy will be done";

But never underneath the sod has God imprisoned anyone.

God does not send disease, or crime,
Or carelessness, or fighting clans;

And when we die before our time the fault is man's.
He is a God of Life not death:

Blame Not God

He is One God that gives birth:

He has not shortened by a breath

The Life of any on this earth.

And He would have us dwell with in

The World our full allotted years.

So blame not God

For our own sin makes our own tears.

CHAPTER 4
WHERE DID DEATH COME FROM?

The first death occurred when Satan and the fallen angels decided to leave their "habitation" and become disembodied spirits:

> *And the angels which kept not their first estate, but left their own habitation, he hath reserved in everlasting chains under darkness unto the judgment of the great day.*
>
> **—Jude 1:6 KJV**

This was, essentially, a massive suicide. When they made this choice, by their gift of free will, they brought the law of sin and death against themselves. Satan knows that in the end he will have to pay his debt to this law in hell.

The first animal sacrifice was made in the Garden of Eden. God used the skins to cover Adam and Eve's naked bodies. But the animal wasn't killed just for clothes; it was a natural illustration to teach them about the way of protection from the law of sin and death they had just put themselves under. When God covered them with the animal skin, it was a natural illustration to teach covering for their sin.

But death wasn't God's idea. He can't stand it and never could. But the law of sin and death required it. (For those of us who love animals, Jewish history records that the sacrifices were performed with no pain to the animal.)

The Scriptures make it clear that God has no pleasure in animal sacrifices:

> *Hear the word of the Lord, ye rulers of Sodom; give ear unto the law of our God, ye people of Gomorrah. To what purpose is the multitude of your sacrifices unto me? saith the Lord: I am full of the burnt offerings of rams, and the fat of fed beasts; and I delight not in the blood of bullocks, or of lambs, or of he goats.*
> **—Isaiah 1:10–11 KJV**

> *O Lord, open thou my lips; and my mouth shall shew forth thy praise. For thou desirest not sacrifice; else would I give it: thou delightest not in burnt offering. The sacrifices of God are a broken spirit: a broken and a contrite heart, O God, thou wilt not despise.*
> **—Psalm 51:15–17 KJV**

David was saying that God did NOT delight in burnt offerings, but a broken and contrite (repentant) heart, meaning a humble spirit before the Lord.

Even the New Testament reminds us God has no pleasure in any of the sacrifices of the Mosaic Law:

> *Above when he said, Sacrifice and offering and burnt offerings and offering for sin thou wouldest not, neither hadst pleasure therein; which are offered by the law.*
>
> **—Hebrews 10:8 KJV**

> *The Lord is not slack concerning his promise, as some men count slackness; but is longsuffering to us-ward, not willing that any should perish, but that all should come to repentance.*
>
> **—2 Peter 3:9 KJV**

We cannot even imagine God's mighty love for us. His very substance is love. If all the human love in this world were put together in one big mass, it would be but a grain of sand compared to the magnificent volume of God's love for you and me. All the sand on the beaches and under the oceans could not measure it.

> *For God so loved the world, that he gave his only begotten Son, that whosoever believeth in him should not perish, but have everlasting life. For God sent not his Son into the world to condemn the world; but that the world through him might be saved. He that believeth on him is not condemned: but he that believeth not is condemned already, because he hath not believed in the name of*

> *the only begotten Son of God.*
> **—John 3:16–18 KJV**

You can see here in some of the most memorized scriptures that God does not condemn. But just what does condemn mean?

Merriam-Webster Dictionary Online / condemn / transitive verb: (1) to declare to be reprehensible, wrong, or evil usually after weighing evidence and without reservation / (2a) to pronounce guilty: convict / (b) sentence, doom.

Merriam-Webster Dictionary Online / sentence / transitive verb: (1) to impose a sentence on / (2) to cause to suffer something.

Merriam-Webster Dictionary Online / sentence / noun: (2a) judgment; specifically: one formally pronounced by a court or judge in a criminal proceeding and specifying the punishment to be inflicted upon the convict / (b) the punishment so imposed.

> *Jesus cried and said, He that believeth on me, believeth not on me, but on him that sent me. And he that seeth me seeth him that sent me. I am come a light [truth] into the world, that whosoever believeth on me should not abide in darkness. And if any man hear my words, and believe not, I judge him not: for I came not to judge the world, but to save the world. He that rejecteth me, and receiveth not my words, hath one that judgeth him: the word*

> *[scripture] that I have spoken, the same shall judge him in the last day.*
> **—John 12:44–48 KJV**

If we are going to be judged by the Word of God at judgment, isn't it a good idea to judge ourselves by the Word of God (Bible) here and now? Scripture says it is the Word of God that chastises us; it is for reproof, correction, instruction, and is a "two-edged sword."

> *All scripture is given by inspiration of God, and is profitable for doctrine, for reproof, for correction, for instruction in righteousness: that the man of God may be perfect, thoroughly furnished unto all good works.*
> **—2 Timothy 3:16–17 KJV**

> *For the word of God is quick, and powerful, and sharper than any two-edged sword, piercing even to the dividing asunder of soul and spirit, and of the joints and marrow, and is a discerner of the thoughts and intents of the heart.*
> **—Hebrews 4:12 KJV**

By man's free will, he condemns himself to hell. One of the most important verses to remember is what Jesus said in John 5:22 KJV: "The Father judgeth no man."

WHAT IS THE LAW OF SIN AND DEATH?

I believe our misinterpretation of the law of sin and death is one of the reasons God's character has been misunderstood for so long. It has created a missing link in our teachings. Even the Old Testament authors thought the law of sin and death and its wrath was God. They did not have the benefit of the Spirit of God joined to their spirit (which began on the Day of Pentecost) to reveal truth to them.

The law of sin and death is one of the three basic laws found in the New Testament. Each of these three laws cannot be fully understood individually without understanding all three and how they work. In fact, when you can grasp the differences in the meanings and functions of these three laws, it is easier to understand the Bible. From Genesis to Revelation, it will not contradict itself. It is also virtually impossible to understand the Book of Romans without the true knowledge of these three laws. They are:

1. The Law of the Spirit of Life

2. The Law of Sin and Death

3. The Mosaic Law

Apostle Paul did not write out the complete names of these laws every time he mentioned them. Maybe it was because he had taught this clearly when he visited those to whom he wrote. Or it could have been the interpreters who deemed it unnecessary to write the full name of each law every time. Whichever is the case, it created havoc for us to understand— until the Holy Spirit gives enlightenment. Both the law of the Spirit of life and the law of sin and death were, however, named in Paul's letter to the Romans:

> *There is therefore now no condemnation to them which are in Christ Jesus, who walk not after the flesh, but after the Spirit. For the law of the Spirit of life in Christ Jesus hath made me free from the law of sin and death. For what the (Mosiac) law could not do, in that it was weak through the flesh, God sending His own Son in the likeness of sinful flesh, and for sin, condemned sin in the flesh: that the righteousness of the law (of the Spirit of Life) might be fulfilled in us, who walk not after the flesh, but after the Spirit. For they that are after the flesh do mind the things of the flesh but they that are after the Spirit the things of the Spirit.*
>
> **—Romans 8:1–5 KJV**

We must lay a foundation of biblical truths to build our theology upon. Isaiah 28:9–10 tells us that we learn God's Word line upon line and precept upon precept; we are "weaned from the milk" or basic understanding of the Word to the deeper truths:

As we have previously seen in Isaiah 28:9-10, which tells us:

> *Whom shall he teach knowledge? and whom shall he make to understand doctrine? them that are weaned from the milk, and drawn from the breasts. For precept must be upon precept, precept upon precept; line upon line, line upon line; here a little, and there a little.*
>
> **—Isaiah 28:9–10 KJV**

Once we are saved, the Holy Spirit will teach and reveal truth to us. Jesus said:

> *But when the Comforter is come, whom I will send unto you from the Father, even the Spirit of truth, which proceedeth from the Father, he shall testify of me.*
>
> **—John 15:26 KJV**

> *But the anointing which ye have received of him abideth in you, and ye need not that any man teach you: but as the same anointing teacheth you of all things, and is truth, and is no lie, and even as it hath taught you, ye shall abide in him.*
>
> **—1 John 2:27 KJV**

So as we study we are to pray the Holy Spirit will reveal truth and understanding. We must always pray for Scripture illumination by the Holy Spirit ,; never just take someone's word, not mine either. Remember it is not your revelation until the Holy Spirit gives it to you, but when He does, you've got it, and no one can take it from you!

Let's take a closer look at the three basic laws taught in the New Testament:

1. The Law of the Spirit of Life

God made covenants (binding agreements) with His angels and mankind. The first known of these was God's covenants of free will and sowing and reaping. These covenants were God's Word in heaven that operated first between God and His angels.

God sowed (gave) love to the angels and, by their free will, they sowed love back to God. (See chart 1.) In heaven the Law of the Spirit of Life was simply sowing and reaping love (by way of free will), which is part of God's character. God reaped the angels' love until Satan rebelled against Him by sowing envy and hate. God didn't think up sin, Satan did. As we saw in chapter 2, God is love (1 John 4:8) and love thinks no evil (1 Corinthians 13:4–5).

As long as these covenants operated on love, they were called the Law of the Spirit of Life. (See charts 2 and 3.) God's intention was for His everlasting covenants of free will and sowing and reaping to operate eternally on everlasting love.

> *The Lord hath appeared of old unto me, saying, Yea, I have loved thee with an everlasting love: therefore with lovingkindness have I drawn thee.*
> **—Jeremiah 31:3 KJV**

2. The Law of Sin and Death

(See chart 4.)

Satan's first transgression—or sin (act of rebellion based on free will)—created the second law: the Law of Sin and Death. God's covenant of sowing and reaping could not be altered or changed. So, since love reaps life, sin had to reap death, or eternal separation from God.

Adam and Eve were created under the Law of Spirit of Life, God's "love law" and Word in heaven, which would later manifest on earth as God's Word in Jesus. (See chart 6.) When they sinned, they put themselves plus all mankind and the whole earth) under the law of sin and death. They had to reap their sin.

Another way to look at what happened in the Garden of Eden and the covenant of sowing and reaping is the popular concept (attributed to Aristotle) of cause and effect or the Buddhist theory of karmaphala (action and result). But actually, King Solomon explained this concept many years before and it is recorded in the Bible:

> *As the bird by wandering, as the swallow by flying, so the curse causeless shall not come.*
> **—Proverbs 26:2 KJV**

Merriam-Webster Dictionary Online / cause / noun: (1a) a reason for an action or condition : motive / (b) something that brings about an effect or a result.

Satan's sin was the cause that created the curse of wrath called the Law of Sin and Death. Before the Law of Sin and Death existed, there was no transgression (sin).

> *Because the law worketh wrath: for where no law is, there is no transgression.*
> **—Romans 4:15 KJV**

There was no sin before Satan transgressed, because he was created perfect in all his ways. He was perfect from the day he was created until iniquity was found in him—until he sinned against God (Ezekiel 28:14–15). This means Satan was not a murderer or a liar when he was created. By his own free will, he chose to transgress, to lead one-third of the angels away from God and persuade them to leave their own "habitation" and become disembodied spirits.

Remember, sin is not a created substance; it is an act of rebellion based on free will.

> *Ye are of your father the devil, and the lusts of your father ye will do. He was a murderer from the beginning [of his sin], and abode not in the truth, because there is no truth in him. When he speaketh a lie, he speaketh of his own: for he is a liar, and the father of it.*
> **—John 8:44 KJV**

Even though Satan was created perfect, the above verse says he did not remain in the truth of God's love. He was a murderer from the beginning of his sin or first act of rebellion.

Satan cursed himself and one-third of the angelic host of heaven who yielded to his lies and followed his advice to leave their first estate (their place, position, or rank in heaven) and their habitation (house, or angelic bodies God created) to become spirits without bodies. Satan, being full of envy and jealousy, wanted to be a spirit like God. He sowed death and bondage along with these angels:

> *And the angels which kept not their first estate, but left their own habitation, he hath reserved in everlasting chains under darkness unto the judgment of the great day.*
>
> **—Jude 1:6 KJV**

Strong's Lexicon / first estate / Greek #746: arche ar-khay': from 756; (properly abstract) a commencement, or (concretely) chief (in various applications of order, time, place, or rank):–beginning, corner, (at the, the) first (estate), magistrate, power, principality, principle, rule.

Strong's Lexicon / habitation / Greek #3613: oiketerion oy-kay-tay'-ree-on: a residence (literally or figuratively):–habitation, house.

The same "cause and effect" happened when Adam and Eve yielded Satan's lies in the Garden. Because God does not condemn and punish, He created Adam to enforce the law of sin and death against Satan and the fallen angels:

> *For the father judgeth no man...*
> **—John 5:22 KJV**

At Calvary—the birth of our salvation—the angels were again made lower than us, just as it was before the fall of Adam and Eve. This gives us back the power over fallen angels, which are called "demonic spirits" or "demons." Scripture instructs us to do what Adam was supposed to do: judge the angels.

> *Know ye not that we shall judge angels? how much more things that pertain to this life?*
> **—1 Corinthians 6:3 KJV**

There is a constant, invisible battle between the principalities in the air above us. The fallen angels fight for our souls, planting lies in our heads. In order to do the works of Christ on this earth, one must put on the whole armor of God, which is His living Word, and join His army:

> *For we wrestle not against flesh and blood, but against principalities, against powers, against the rulers of the darkness of this world, against spiritual wickedness in high places. Wherefore take unto you the whole armour of God, that ye may be able to withstand in the evil day, and having done all, to stand. Stand therefore, having your loins girt about with truth, and having on the breastplate of righteousness; And your feet shod with the preparation of the gospel of peace; Above*

> *all, taking the shield of faith, wherewith ye shall be able to quench all the fiery darts of the wicked. And take the helmet of salvation, and the sword of the Spirit, which is the word of God.*
>
> **—Ephesians 6:12–17 KJV**

By divine partnership—Jesus in us, praying through us—we are to command the devil to flee from us:

> *Submit yourselves therefore to God. Resist the devil, and he will flee from you.*
>
> **—James 4:7 KJV**

The law of sin and death is a "cause and effect" of Satan's transgression of the law of the Spirit of life. So Satan created it and Adam and Eve's transgression put the whole world under it. God had created a perfect world without sin, sickness, or death. This brings us to the third law, the Mosaic Law, which will be covered in the next chapter.

CHAPTER 5

WHAT IS THE MOSAIC LAW?

The Mosaic Law contained rules of moral conduct called the Ten Commandments. It also included special rituals and animal sacrifices that were required by the law of sin and death. These rules were set forth in the first five books of the Old Testament, called the Torah.

The Mosaic Law was given by God to the children of Israel, but anyone who would receive it could reap its benefits. God is no respecter of persons—He doesn't favor one of us over others—and He always makes a way of escape.

The Mosaic Law had two main purposes:

1. To act as a covering or protection from the law of sin and death so mankind wouldn't have to reap the consequence of their sins <u>while on this earth</u>.

2. To be a schoolmaster—an instructor to teach about the law of sin and death, the covenant of sowing and reaping and how it operated.

I call the Mosaic Law with its Ten Commandments a "love law"—a gift from God to mankind until Jesus would come to replace it.

The Ten Commandments are found in Exodus:

And God spake all these words, saying, I am the Lord thy God, which have brought thee out of the land of Egypt, out of the house of bondage. [1] Thou shalt have no other gods before me. [2] Thou shalt not make unto thee any graven image, or any likeness of any thing that is in heaven above, or that is in the earth beneath, or that is in the water under the earth . . . [3] Thou shalt not take the name of the Lord thy God in vain; for the Lord will not hold him guiltless that taketh his name in vain. [4] Remember the sabbath day, to keep it holy. Six days shalt thou labour, and do all thy work: but the seventh day is the sabbath of the Lord thy God: in it thou shalt not do any work, . . . [5] Honour thy father and thy mother: that thy days may be long upon the land which the Lord thy God giveth thee. [6] Thou shalt not kill. [7] Thou shalt not commit adultery. [8] Thou shalt not steal. [9] Thou shalt not bear false witness against thy neighbour. [10] Thou shalt not covet thy neighbour's house, thou shalt not covet thy neighbour's wife, nor his manservant, nor

> *his maidservant, nor his ox, nor his ass, nor any thing that is thy neighbour's. And all the people saw the thunderings, and the lightnings, and the noise of the trumpet, and the mountain smoking: and when the people saw it, they removed, and stood afar off . . . And Moses said unto the people, Fear not: for God is come to prove you, and that his fear may be before your faces, that ye sin not. And the people stood afar off, and Moses drew near unto the thick darkness where God was. And the Lord said unto Moses, Thus thou shalt say unto the children of Israel, Ye have seen that I have talked with you from heaven.*
> **—Exodus 20:1–4, 7–10, 12–18, 20–22 KJV**

But what were the animal sacrifices all about? As we discussed in chapter 2, the law of sin and death required bloodshed and death. (It is worth noting that God gave detailed instructions for every sacrifice to ensure the death of the animals would be instant and painless. These instructions were handed down orally through the rabbis from generation to generation. These oral commentaries were eventually written down and compiled into the Mishnah, which today can be found translated into the English language. God's loving and compassionate character can be seen clearly in a study of the Mishnah.

> *There hath no temptation taken you but such as is common to man: but God is faithful, who will not suffer you to be tempted above*

> *that ye are able; but will with the temptation also make a way to escape, that ye may be able to bear it.*
>
> **—1 Corinthians 10:13 KJV**

Do people sin? Do even Christians mess up and sin? Of course we do. But the above verse shows us that with every temptation from the devil, God has provided an escape. Through Jesus and His Word, we have been given the power to resist the devil's lies by cutting off the mental images of temptation before they can evolve into action (sin).

In chapter 3, we established that God has no pleasure in the death of anyone:

> *For I have no pleasure in the death of him that dieth, saith the Lord God: wherefore turn yourselves, and live ye.*
>
> **—Ezekiel 18:32KJV**

> *Say unto them, As I live, saith the Lord God, I have no pleasure in the death of the wicked; but that the wicked turn from his way and live: turn ye, turn ye from your evil ways; for why will ye die, O house of Israel?*
>
> **—Ezekiel 33:11 KJV**

God is light, love, and life. He wants us to choose life! He says in Deuteronomy 30:19–20 KJV:

I have set before you life and death, blessing and

cursing: therefore choose life, that both thou and thy seed may live: That thou mayest love the Lord thy God, and that thou mayest obey his voice, and that thou mayest cleave unto him: for he is thy life.

The Mosaic Law was to be a schoolmaster to lead us to life:

> *But the scripture hath concluded all under sin, that the promise by faith of Jesus Christ might be given to them that believe. But before faith [Jesus Christ] came, we were kept under the law [Mosaic Law], shut up unto the faith which should afterwards be revealed. Wherefore the law was our schoolmaster to bring us unto Christ, that we might be justified by faith. But after that faith is come, we are no longer under a schoolmaster. For ye are all the children of God by faith in Christ Jesus.*
> **—Galatians 3:22–26 KJV**

Strong's Lexicon / kept / Greek #5432: phroureo froo-reh'-o: from a compound of 4253 and 3708; to be a watcher in advance, i.e. to mount guard as a sentinel (post spies at gates); figuratively, to hem in, protect:– keep (with a garrison). Compare 5083.

In order to understand the Scriptures, we must know and recognize the difference between each of the three laws found in the Bible:

> *For the law of the Spirit of life in Christ Jesus hath made me free from the law of sin and death.*
>
> **—Romans 8:2 KJV**

In most of Paul's letters, which became many of the books of the New Testament, he speaks often about these three laws:

1. Law of the Spirit of life

2. Law of sin and death (also called "wrath")

3. Mosaic Law

Many teachers today don't know the difference between the Mosaic Law and the law of sin and death. They believe they are the same law, which makes for confused scripture and fal- lacy in our Christian doctrine.

Before Christ came, people had to die for their own sin. It was an eye for an eye and a tooth for a tooth.

> *But every one shall die for his own iniquity: every man that eateth the sour grape, his teeth shall be set on edge.*
>
> **—Jeremiah 31:30 KJV**

> *And if any mischief follow, then thou shalt give life for life, eye for eye, tooth for tooth, hand for hand, foot for foot, burning for burning, wound for wound, stripe for stripe.*
>
> **—Exodus 21:23–25 KJV**

But notice that the next verse (Jeremiah 31:31) is a prophecy of God's new covenant with man. It says that God will put His Word in the hearts of His children (join His Spirit with ours at salvation) and that this new covenant will take the place of the old one. The Mosaic Law will be in our hearts and the sacrifices and rituals will be replaced by His law of the Spirit of life through Jesus Christ. And the sins of mankind will not be remembered:

> *Behold, the days come, saith the Lord, that I will make a new covenant with the house of Israel, and with the house of Judah: Not according to the covenant that I made with their fathers in the day that I took them by the hand to bring them out of the land of Egypt; which my covenant they brake, although I was an husband unto them, saith the Lord: But this shall be the covenant that I will make with the house of Israel; After those days, saith the Lord, I will put my law in their inward parts, and write it in their hearts; and will be their God, and they shall be my people. And they shall teach no more every man his neighbour, and every man his brother, saying, Know the Lord: for they shall all know me, from the least of them unto the greatest of them, saith the Lord: for I will forgive their iniquity, and I will remember their sin no more.*
>
> **—Jeremiah 31:31–34 KJV**

The new covenant came in Jesus Christ and becomes our way of life when His Spirit joins to ours. Old Testament law (Exodus 21:23–25) instructs to give a life for a life and an eye for an eye. But in the New Testament, Jesus referred to the Mosaic Law saying:

> *Ye have heard that it hath been said, An eye for an eye, and a tooth for a tooth: but I say unto you, That ye resist not evil: but whosoever shall smite thee on thy right cheek, turn to him the other also. And if any man will sue thee at the law, and take away thy coat, let him have thy cloak also. And whosoever shall compel thee to go a mile, go with him twain. Give to him that asketh thee, and from him that would borrow of thee turn not thou away. Ye have heard that it hath been said, Thou shalt love thy neighbour, and hate thine enemy. But I say unto you, Love your enemies, bless them that curse you, do good to them that hate you, and pray for them which despitefully use you, and persecute you.*
>
> **—Matthew 5:38–44 KJV**

The Mosaic Law could not take away sins nor give eternal life:

> *For it is not possible that the blood of bulls and of goats should take away sins. Wherefore when he cometh into the world, he saith, Sacrifice and offering thou wouldest not, but a body hast thou prepared me: In*

> *burnt offerings and sacrifices for sin thou hast had no pleasure. Then said I [Jesus], Lo, I come (in the volume of the book it is written of me,) to do thy will, O God. Above when he said, Sacrifice and offering and burnt offerings and offering for sin thou wouldest not, neither hadst pleasure therein; which are offered by the law [Mosaic Law]; Then said he, Lo, I come to do thy will, O God. He taketh away the first, that he may establish the second. By the which will we are sanctified through the offering of the body of Jesus Christ once for all. And every priest standeth daily ministering and offering oftentimes the same sacrifices, which can never take away sins: But this man, after he had offered one sacrifice for sins for ever, sat down on the right hand of God.*
>
> **—Hebrews 10:4–12 KJV**

In Jesus Christ, we don't have to reap death (eternal separation from God); we don't have to pay the high price for our sins. Jesus paid that price at Calvary for every human being. But under the old Mosaic Law, sins were remembered and sacrifices made over and over every year for those same sins:

> *For the law having a shadow of good things to come, and not the very image of the things, can never with those sacrifices which they offered year by year continually make the comers thereunto perfect. For then would*

> *they not have ceased to be offered? because that the worshippers once purged should have had no more conscience of sins. But in those sacrifices there is a remembrance again made of sins every year.*
>
> **—Hebrews 10:1–3 KJV**

When Jesus forgives us, our sins are remembered no more:

> *And I will remember their sin no more.*
>
> **—Jeremiah 31:34 KJV**

But it is up to our free will to ask Christ for forgiveness and receive His precious salvation. Then and only then are our sins forgiven and never remembered again . . . ever. Through Christ we are placed back under the protection of the law of the Spirit of life, which includes the two most important laws of God from which all other laws come. They are to love God with all your heart and to love your neighbor as yourself—sowing and reaping love!

> *But God commendeth his love toward us, in that, while we were yet sinners, Christ died for us. Much more then, being now justified by his blood, we shall be saved from wrath [Law of Sin and Death] through him.*
>
> **—Romans 5:8–9 KJV**

> *For the wages of sin is death; but the gift of God is eternal life through Jesus Christ our Lord.*
> **—Romans 6:23 NIV**

> *That whosoever believeth in him should not perish, but have eternal life. For God so loved the world, that he gave his only begotten Son, that whosoever believeth in him should not perish, but have everlasting life. For God sent not his Son into the world to condemn the world; but that the world through him might be saved.*
> **—John 3:15–17 KJV**

We have learned that the Mosaic Law, given to Moses by God, was to protect mankind from the wrath of the law of sin and death, from having to reap the consequences of their sins. It was also an instructor and teacher of that which was to come. It was meant to point us to the coming once and for all protection from eternal death, Jesus Christ.

Scriptures are clear that the Mosaic Law was not enough to save or redeem man from sin eternally. So when did all those who died before Christ have the opportunity to receive their eternal salvation? Read the answer in chapter 10, "The Rest of the Easter Story."

CHAPTER 6

WHAT REALLY HAPPENED IN THE GARDEN?

I think most of us are curious about what happened in the Garden of Eden and have many unanswered questions. Many new Christians think they need to start at the beginning of the Bible, to start reading it like you would any other book. My grandson Hunter wrote me from military boot camp and said, "I have started reading the Bible, but the first three chapters of Genesis bother me a lot."

To most it seems like a fairy tale or parable with some sort of meaning behind it that they can't quite figure out. Most ask how eating a fruit could make you a sinner. What kind of God has wrath toward His own creation? God couldn't have loved Adam and Eve or He wouldn't have put them out of the Garden, right? Wrong.

The truth is, this is not what happened in the Garden.

It is next to impossible to understand this chapter without understanding the first four chapters of this book, for they are the foundation. We learn line upon line and precept upon precept. Having a solid foundation of truth is the most important.

> *Whom shall he teach knowledge? and whom shall he make to understand doctrine? them that are weaned from the milk, and drawn from the breasts. For precept must be upon precept, precept upon precept; line upon line, line upon line; here a little, and there a little.*
>
> **—Isaiah 28:9–10**

I believe a new Christian should read what Jesus taught first to get a true foundation of God's character, because the whole Bible must line up with what Jesus taught or we have the wrong interpretation. The Book of John is a great first read:

> *In the beginning was the Word, and the Word was with God, and the Word was God. The same was in the beginning with God. All things were made by him; and without him was not any thing made that was made. In him was life; and the life was the light of men. And the light shineth in darkness; and the darkness comprehended it not.*
>
> **—John 1:1–5 KJV**

> *He was in the world, and the world was made by him, and the world knew him not . . . And the Word was made flesh, and dwelt among us, (and we beheld his glory, the glory*

> *as of the only begotten of the Father,) full of grace and truth . . . For the law was given by Moses, but grace and truth came by Jesus Christ.*
>
> **—John 1:10, 14, 17 KJV**

Jesus was God's Word that spoke the universe into existence.

> *If ye had known me, ye should have known my Father also: and from henceforth ye know him, and have seen him. Philip saith unto him, Lord, shew us the Father, and it sufficeth us. Jesus saith unto him, Have I been so long time with you, and yet hast thou not known me, Philip? he that hath seen me hath seen the Father; and how sayest thou then, Shew us the Father? Believest thou not that I am in the Father, and the Father in me? the words that I speak unto you I speak not of myself: but the Father that dwelleth in me, he doeth the works.*
>
> **—John 14:7–10 KJV**

It is very important to know that, like the Book of Revelation, Genesis 1–3 is not completely in chronological order. As an example: Genesis 1:26 records the creation of Adam and Eve, but the details of making woman are in Genesis 2:21–23:

> *And the Lord God caused a deep sleep to fall upon Adam, and he slept: and he took one*

of his ribs, and closed up the flesh instead thereof; And the rib, which the Lord God had taken from man, made he a woman, and brought her unto the man. And Adam said, This is now bone of my bones, and flesh of my flesh: she shall be called Woman, because she was taken out of Man.

—Genesis 2:21–23 KJV

Strong's Lexicon / rib / Hebrew #6763: tsela` tsay-law' or (feminine) tsalTah {tsal-aw'}; from 6760; a rib (as curved), literally (of the body) or figuratively (of a door, i.e. leaf); hence, a side, literally (of a person) or figuratively (of an object or the sky, i.e. quarter); architecturally, a (especially floor or ceiling) timber or plank (single or collective, i.e. a flooring):–beam, board, chamber, corner, leaf, plank, rib, side (chamber).

It's interesting that the meaning of the original Hebrew word for "rib" actually refers to a curve. I believe this is a reference to the curve of human DNA. Thus, this is saying that Eve was not formed from a rib (bone) from Adam's side but from his DNA. This makes a lot of sense. When the Bible was translated into English, we did not know about DNA, so the interpreters got the wrong English word for the meaning of the Hebrew word. Look at all the curves and arcs within the picture of the DNA below:

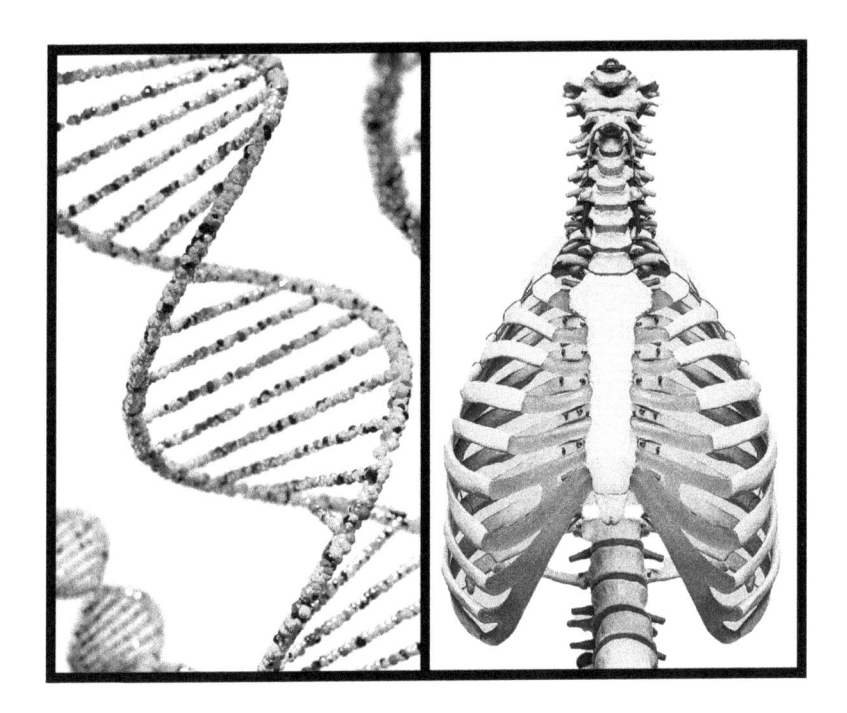

The word helix comes from the Greek word meaning "twisted or curved." Helices are important in biology, as the DNA molecule is formed as two intertwined helices and many proteins have helical substructures.

Look at our curved DNA above. Doesn't it make sense that God made Eve from Adam's DNA?

> *And Adam said, This is now bone of my bones, and flesh of my flesh: she shall be called Woman, because she was taken out of Man.*
>
> **—Genesis 2:23 KJV**

COMMON MISCONCEPTIONS ABOUT THE GARDEN OF EDEN

1. The fruit that Adam and Eve ate was not literally an edible fruit, but the fruit of evil.

An example of this symbolism is in Hosea, when sin is referred to as "eating the fruit of lies." Israel was full of sin and rebellion against God and was worshiping manmade images (pagan gods), but God was always trying to turn them around; to protect them so they wouldn't have to reap the wrath of the Law of Sin and Death.

> *Sow to yourselves in righteousness, reap in mercy; break up your fallow ground: for it is time to seek the Lord, till he come and rain righteousness upon you. Ye have plowed wickedness, ye have reaped iniquity; ye have eaten the fruit of lies: because thou didst trust in thy way, in the multitude of thy mighty men.*
>
> **—Hosea 10:12–13 KJV**

When did Eve sin? She sinned when she ate the fruit of lies and repeated Lucifer's lie. When she spoke the lie, she acknowledged to Adam that she believed Lucifer's words when he said, "God has lied to you. You shall not surely die." Eve spoke blasphemy toward God. It was a lie!

> *For as in Adam all die, even so in Christ shall all be made alive.*
>
> **—1 Corinthians 15:22 KJV**

WHAT REALLY HAPPENED IN THE GARDEN?

Her sin pushed God's Spirit away from her spirit. Because of God's covenant of free will and sowing and reaping, Eve's sin took her out from under God's law of the Spirit of life and put her under the law of sin and death, which brought sickness, pain, and physical death. But God's plan was for man to live forever.

> *And the serpent [a symbol of Lucifer] said unto the woman, Ye shall not surely die: For God doth know that in the day ye eat thereof, then your eyes shall be opened, and ye shall be as gods, knowing good and evil.*
> **—Genesis 3:4–5 KJV**

When did Adam sin? He sinned when he ate of the fruit of lies by speaking in agreement with Eve.

> *Thou art snared with the words of thy mouth, thou art taken with the words of thy mouth.*
> **—Proverbs 6:2 KJV**

He probably said something like our husbands would after we have influenced them. "Yeah, babe. That sounds good. I think you're right."

> *Death and life are in the power of the tongue: and they that love it shall eat the fruit thereof.*
> **—Proverbs 18:21 NIV**

> *Know ye not, that to whom ye yield yourselves servants to obey, his servants ye are to whom*

> *ye obey; whether of sin unto death, or of obedience unto righteousness?*
>
> **—Romans 6:16 KJV**

The moment Eve heard Satan's lies in her mind she should have gone to God first before she repeated the lies to Adam. She should have asked God, "What about these thoughts in my head that say You have not told us the truth? Lord, teach me truth." Likewise, Adam should not have believed and accepted Eve's fruit of lies, repeating them before going to God asking Him, "God, what about this? Where did this come from? What is going on here? Lord, teach me truth."

Teachers, we should never repeat some other man's interpretation of Scripture until we have first asked God (the Holy Spirit) in us to teach us truth. And when we are being taught by another, we should never repeat the revelations we learn until the Holy Spirit—our ultimate teacher—has revealed truth to us. No wonder our modern theology has a confused message! It has man's intellect woven into it instead of truth from the pure Word revealed by the Holy Spirit.

> *When we look at the original Hebrew words of the Old Testament, we can see clearly that God had a specific job for mankind to do: And God blessed them, and God said unto them, Be fruitful, and multiply, and replenish the earth, and subdue it: and have dominion over the fish of the sea, and over*

the fowl of the air, and over every living thing that moveth upon the earth.

—Genesis 1:28 KJV

Strong's Lexicon / dominion / Hebrew #7287: radah raw-daw' a primitive root; to tread down, i.e. subjugate; specifically, to crumble off:–(come to, make to) have dominion, prevail against, reign, (bear, make to) rule,(- r, over), take.

Merriam-Webster Dictionary Online / dominion / noun: (1) domain / (2) supreme authority.

Strong's Lexicon / subdue / Hebrew #3533: kabash kaw-bash' a primitive root; to tread down; hence, negatively, to disregard; positively, to conquer, subjugate, violate:– bring into bondage, force, keep under, subdue, bring into subjection.

Merriam-Webster Dictionary Online / subdue / transi- tive verb: to conquer and bring into subjection : vanquish / (2) to bring under control especially by an exertion of the will . . . / (4) to reduce the intensity or degree of : tone down.

So who were Adam and Eve to subdue? The very reason God created them was to do something that He (deity) could not do: judge the angels (specifically demons), enforce the law of sin and death on Satan and his demonic forces (fallen angels). God had given Adam and Eve power over all the principalities of the air. But the first Adam failed to subdue, giving away dominion of the earth to Satan.

Before man's sin, the animals did not even kill for food. Adam, Eve, and the animals were vegetarian and ate God's organic food; perfect in color, taste, and smell and so full of all of the nutrients that their self-healing bodies needed to live forever.

2. The serpent was not a literal snake.

The snake in the Garden was a symbol for Satan. God has always used natural illustrations, symbols, and parables to teach mankind. In scripture, Satan is known as Lucifer, the devil, and Beelzebub (the chief or prince of devils). But the symbols for him are serpent, snake, and dragon.

> *And the great dragon was cast out [at Calvary], that old serpent [in Genesis], called the Devil, and Satan, which deceiveth the whole world: he was cast out into the earth, and his angels were cast out with him.*
> **—Revelation 12:9 KJV**

(Also see chapter 12, "When Was the War in Heaven?") Why did God use a serpent for a symbol of illustration?

God was speaking to Moses, the writer of Genesis, who did not have God's Spirit joined to his for understanding. So God was using an illustration Moses could relate to: the characteristics of a snake, just like Jesus used the characteristics of a mother hen who gathered her baby chicks up under her wings to protect them. Some theologians might try to figure out what kind of feathers and how many, when all God wants us to do is accept the simple natural illustrations He is presenting, "Oh Israel, I would have protected you."

> *O Jerusalem, Jerusalem, thou that killest the prophets, and stonest them which are sent unto thee, how often would I have gathered thy children together, even as a hen gathereth her chickens under her wings, and ye would not!*
>
> **—Matthew 23:37 KJV**

Moses lived in a desert where there were deadly serpents that were the same color as the dirt and were therefore very hard to see. They could sneak up on you and you wouldn't even see them. This is a great illustration of Satan and how he sneaks up on mankind with temptations.

3. The trees were not literal trees. They were trees of illustration.

Image 2 Keith Porter's picture of the 2 trees in the garden and what they *represent*

The tree of life represented the law of the Spirit of life. God's Word and God's Spirit in us brings everlasting life. The Book of Revelation refers to the law of the Spirit of life in heaven as the same symbol: the tree of life—the fruit of God—which we will eat of one day.

> *He that hath an ear, let him hear what the Spirit saith unto the churches; To him that*

> *overcometh will I give to eat of the tree of life, which is in the midst of the paradise of God.*
> **—Revelation 2:7 KJV**

> *Blessed are they that do his commandments, that they may have right to the tree of life, and may enter in through the gates into the city.*
> **—Revelation 22:14 KJV**

The tree of the knowledge of good and evil represented the law of sin and death. Scripture confirms that life is a blessing (good) and death is a curse (evil):

> *I call heaven and earth to record this day against you, that I have set before you life and death, blessing and cursing: therefore choose life, that both thou and thy seed may live.*
> **—Deuteronomy 30:19 KJV**

There is not a fairy tale of magical trees in Genesis. God had already told them the fruit of every seed-yielding tree was for their food so this tree of the knowledge of good and evil couldn't have been one of those literal, physical trees:

> *And God said, Behold, I have given you every herb bearing seed, which is upon the face of all the earth, and every tree, in the which is the fruit of a tree yielding seed; to you it shall be for meat. And to every beast of the earth,*

> *and to every fowl of the air, and to every thing that creepeth upon the earth, wherein there is life, I have given every green herb for meat: and it was so. And God saw every thing that he had made, and, behold, it was very good. And the evening and the morning were the sixth day.*
>
> **—Genesis 1:29–31 KJV**

We don't have a problem with Jesus calling Himself a vine and calling us branches.

> *Abide in me, and I in you. As the branch cannot bear fruit of itself, except it abide in the vine; no more can ye except ye abide in me. I am the vine, ye are the branches: He that abideth in me, and I in him, the same bringeth forth much fruit: for without me ye can do nothing.*
>
> **—John 15:4–5 KJV**

So we shouldn't have trouble with understanding the symbolism of the trees either.

4. The "flaming sword" in Genesis 3:24 was not a literal sword.

> *So he drove out the man; and he placed at the east of the garden of Eden Cherubims, and a flaming sword which turned every way, to keep the way of the tree of life.*
>
> **—Genesis 3:24 KJV**

The flaming sword is a symbol for God's Word or covenant of free will and sowing and reaping, just as the sword of the Spirit represents the truth of God's Word:

> *And take the helmet of salvation, and the sword of the Spirit, which is the word of God.*
> **—Ephesians 6:17 KJV**

The sword represented God's covenant (Word), His intended law of love or law of free will and sowing and reaping.

Now we can see just how important the first three chapters of Genesis really are. It was not a children's fairy tale of a snake talking in a garden with magical trees. No wonder the "theory" of evolution was so easily accepted in our universities over the real creation story in Genesis.

5. Clothing Adam and Eve in animal skins was about far more than just clothing their physical bodies.

Through His non-forsaking, never-failing love for His creation, God figured out a way to protect Adam and Eve from having to reap their sin. He protected them from the law of sin and death.

> *Unto Adam also and to his wife did the Lord God make coats of skins, and clothed them.*
> **—Genesis 3:21 KJV**

I believe this was the first blood sacrifice made unto the law of sin and death. God was teaching them about the covering that would protect them from having to reap their own sins.

Covering them with coats of skin was God's loving and gentle way of teaching them about this temporary way of escaping the enforcement of the law of sin and death: a natural illustration showing the coming Mosaic Law rituals, as well as Jesus Christ, the once and for all atonement for all sin. This was not a picture of a mad or angry God, but of the never- changing God of love.

> *Every good gift and every perfect gift is from above, and cometh down from the Father of lights, with whom is no variableness, neither shadow of turning.*
> **—James 1:17 KJV**

CHAPTER 7
WHAT CAUSED NOAH'S FLOOD

What about the people of Noah's day? If God didn't kill them, who did? Who condemned the world and all those in it with the Flood? Let's look at scripture to find out:

> *By faith Noah, being warned of God of things not seen as yet, moved with fear, prepared an ark to the saving of his house; by the which he condemned the world, and became heir of the righteousness which is by faith.*
>
> **—Hebrews 11:7 KJV**

> *And [God] spared not the old world, but saved Noah the eighth person, a preacher of righteousness, bringing in the flood upon the world of the ungodly.*
>
> **—2 Peter 2:5 KJV**

As we know, the law of sin and death came forth out of God's love law of free will and sowing and reaping. When Satan and his fallen angels perverted God's love law by returning hate, envy, and jealousy back to God, they created sin and the curse and the judgment of the law of sin and death. Because of God's eternal law of sowing and reaping, now the law of sin and death demanded judgment and death for all sin. (See chart 6.) God did not create sin, death, or judgment; they were not in His thoughts and plans. Adam's and Eve's sin put the world and all of mankind in subjection to the law of sin and death.

> *Nevertheless death reigned from Adam to Moses, even over them that had not sinned after the similitude of Adam's transgression, who is the figure of him that was to come.*
>
> **—Romans 5:14 KJV**

No one could cast evil spirits out of people until Jesus Christ came casting them out and giving His disciples that same power:

> *When the even was come, they brought unto him [Jesus] many that were possessed with devils: and he cast out the spirits with his word, and healed all that were sick.*
>
> **—Matthew 8:16 KJV**

> *These twelve Jesus sent forth, and commanded them, saying, Go not into the way of the Gentiles, and into any city of the Samaritans enter ye not: But go rather to the lost sheep of the house of Israel. And as ye go, preach saying, The kingdom of heaven*

> *is at hand. Heal the sick, cleanse the lepers, raise the dead, cast out devils: freely ye have received, freely give.*
>
> **—Matthew 10:5–8 KJV**

In the Old Testament the body (temple) of a person, animal, or thing possessed by an evil spirit had to be destroyed because there wasn't any way to cast them out. Adam and Eve lost the authority over the fallen angels when they bowed their knee to Satan, believed his lies, and repeated them. Thus, Noah didn't have the authority or power to deliver the people from these fallen angels. If they had believed this preacher's words and prophecy, they would have used his blueprints and built many arks.

Because of Noah's prayers concerning this wicked human race, the law of sin and death was enforced on all who refused to believe God's Word and warning of the huge natural disaster that was about to destroy all living things by water (except those on the ark). Those who were filled with evil and demons had opened the door for Satan to destroy them; being under the law of sin and death, they had to reap what they had sown:

> *The thief cometh not, but for to steal, and to kill, and to destroy: I am come that they might have life, and that they might have it more abundantly.*
>
> **—John 10:10 KJV**

God saw what was about to happen and, as always, He provided a way of escape:

> *For I am the Lord, I change not; therefore ye sons of Jacob are not consumed.*
>
> **—Malachi 3:6 KJV**

> *The Lord is not slack concerning his promise, as some men count slackness; but is longsuffering to us-ward, not willing that any should perish, but that all should come to repentance.*
>
> **—2 Peter 3:9 KJV**

> *There hath no temptation taken you but such as is common to man: but God is faithful, who will not suffer you to be tempted above that ye are able; but will with the temptation also make a way to escape, that ye may be able to bear it.*
>
> **—1 Corinthians 10:13 KJV**

The way of escape God provided was a blueprint of an ark that would survive the coming destruction of the Flood.

The concept of a boat was not new to the people of the earth. It is believed that all mankind at that time in history lived along the Tigris and Euphrates Rivers. They had full knowledge of shipbuilding, and the earth was still like the Garden of Eden with plenty of trees for the material needed for the construction of boats. They could have all built a smaller duplicate of Noah's ark for their own place of safety. I believe our God of love wanted to see thousands of arks floating on the floodwaters.

God gave the blueprint for the ark to Noah. As a preacher of righteousness, he shared the word of the Lord. If you knew a flood was coming and you had the only blueprint of a boat that wouldn't sink in the coming storm, don't you think you would say: "Hey, you need to build a boat like this! Here is a way of escape"?

Jesus is our ark of safety from the law of sin and death (Romans 8:1–2). But you can't survive on anyone else's relationship with Jesus. You must build your own relationship with Him.

If the people of Noah's day had heeded Noah's warning and built their own ark, I believe the evil spirits would have had to leave them, just as when Jesus enters our heart and becomes our ark of safety, evil spirits have to leave us:

> *That if thou shalt confess with thy mouth the Lord Jesus, and shalt believe in thine heart that God hath raised him from the dead, thou shalt be saved. For with the heart man believeth unto righteousness; and with the mouth confession is made unto salvation.*
>
> **—Romans 10:9–10 KJV**

CAN GOD KILL?

Moses, the author of Genesis, did not know the difference between God and the law of sin and death, and he did not know God's true character (which Jesus came to reveal). He called the law of sin and death and God one and the same. Thus Moses said God killed and destroyed. But we have seen in Scripture that God did not create death and it is definitely not God's will. God is the giver of life.

Jesus did not die as a sacrifice to God, but willingly gave Himself as a sacrifice to the wrath of the law of sin and death so we could have eternal life in heaven in His holy presence. When we receive Jesus Christ as our Lord and Savior, we are protected under the law of the Spirit of life and will not reap our past sins in the final death (separation from God).

You may wonder, "If God could not have caused or stopped the Flood, how could He promise there would not be another one that would destroy the whole earth again?" Even scientists say that there is not enough water to create another flood to cover the earth. Before Noah's Flood, plant life was watered by a mist from beneath like a huge terrarium. God had made a perfect tropical paradise with a firmament of water like a ring around the earth:

> *And God said, Let there be a firmament in the midst of the waters, and let it divide the waters from the waters. And God made the*

firmament, and divided the waters which were under the firmament from the waters which were above the firmament: and it was so. And God called the firmament Heaven. And the evening and the morning were the second day.

—Genesis 1:6–8 NIV

So when did all those who died in the Flood hear the gospel of Christ for their choice of repentance? You'll find the answer in chapter 11, "The Rest of the Easter Story."

CHAPTER 8

THE TRUTH ABOUT GOD IN THE BOOK OF JOB

I have heard many people, from the pulpits to laymen, use the story of Job to support their theories on God's character and use Job's words to prove that bad circumstances are God just trying to teach us something.

Job lived in the time of the Old Testament, far before Jesus came with the truth about God. So of course Job blamed God for the tragedy in his life. But there are some surprises we're going to look at in God's conversation with Job, right before Job was healed, that may show you the opposite is true. Job was a servant of God, probably the most righteous man at that time and definitely the wealthiest in that part of the country. And even though the book (which Job wrote) says he was a perfect man, you and I know that no human being has ever been truly perfect except Jesus Christ. At some point Satan went to God claiming his right to enforce the law of sin and death on Job and mankind, the law Adam and Eve put man under. Look at Job's words:

> *For the thing which I greatly feared is come upon me, and that which I was afraid of is come unto me.*
>
> **—Job 3:25 KJV**

What does the Bible say about fear?

> *There is no fear in love; but perfect love casteth out fear: because fear hath torment. He that feareth is not made perfect in love.*
>
> **—1 John 4:18 KJV**

> *He that diggeth a pit shall fall into it; and whoso breaketh an hedge, a serpent shall bite him.*
>
> **—Ecclesiastes 10:8 KJV**

Job's fears let down his own hedge of protection. Satan attacked the areas where Job was afraid. But Satan could not take Job's life because Job did not fear dying. Job prayed to die. Job said:

> *So that my soul chooseth strangling, and death rather than my life.*
>
> **—Job 7:15 KJV**

Job continually blamed God for all his troubles; he didn't know the difference between God and the law of sin and death. Job had no knowledge or understanding of God's covenant of free will and sowing and reaping. Nor did he know that Satan was enforcing the law of sin and death on him. He thought God was behind all his bad circumstances. Does this sound familiar in today's Christian world? But we have no excuse; we have Christ's Words to teach us.

The following are Job's words (not God's Words), which lack understanding:

> *And said, Naked came I out of my mother's womb, and naked shall I return thither: the Lord gave, and the Lord hath taken away; blessed be the name of the Lord.*
> **—Job 1:21 KJV**

God does not give us gifts then take them away. The only things He takes away are our sins.

> *For the gifts and calling of God are without repentance.*
> **—Romans 11:29 KJV**

This means we can't get rid of them; they are with us for life. Job admits he was full of confusion:

> *If I be wicked, woe unto me; and if I be righteous, yet will I not lift up my head. I am full of confusion; there- fore see thou mine affliction.*
> **—Job 10:15 KJV**

Satan has hidden himself behind his deception: the fable in our Christian doctrine. Satan has stolen God's miracles long enough. How can someone receive healing if they think God gave them the illness to teach something? Or, even worse, that it is their appointed time to die!

As we studied the scriptures in the first chapters of this book, we discovered that it was Adam and Eve who appointed us to death, not God. But the theory of an appointed time to die has some problems. For instance, what about when a drunk driver kills someone in an accident? Did God need the driver to get drunk and drive just because it was the victim's appointed time to die? What about the murders and illnesses of the babies and children who have been given gifts and talents to use for God and have things to do that no one else can do? Would God snap them out (or allow them to be snapped out) before they even get a chance in life?

All these misconceptions make me want to be a lawyer for God! Was it really the appointed time for everyone who died on September 11, 2001? It may sound ridiculous to you, but I have actually heard some preachers say that it was! So now the terrorists work for God?

We have no excuse; Jesus has come with the truth about God. We have God's own Words spoken by Jesus, printed in red in many Bibles, and written by the hand of some of His disciples who were eyewitnesses. Now there is no more covering; after Christ, we are all held accountable. The truth is in the Word of God. We must seek it out through the Holy Spirit and prayer.

Job wasn't afraid to die. This is why God told Satan he couldn't touch Job's life. In his misery, he longed to die.

> *Which long for death, but it cometh not; and dig for it more than for hid treasures; which rejoice exceedingly, and are glad, when they can find the grave?*
> **—Job 3:21–22 KJV**

As we have studied, no one knew God's true character until Jesus came to reveal Him. Job blamed God for all the tribulations of life. His lack of knowledge gave him the wrong attitude, which made it harder for God to help him. If we don't pray the truth of God's Word, our prayers are just vain words. Job's words were mostly self-pity and were in vain, until he realized he was wrong and repented.

It is sad to me that most teachers have failed to see the end of the Book of Job, when God told Job out of a whirlwind, "Do you condemn Me that you may be righteous?"

> *Then answered the Lord unto Job out of the whirlwind, and said, Gird up thy loins now like a man: I will demand of thee, and declare thou unto me. Wilt thou also disannul my judgment? wilt thou condemn me, that thou mayest be righteous?*
> **—Job 40:6–8 KJV**

When Job admitted his lack of knowledge and repented, God was able to bless him and turn his captivity around.

When Job took his mind off himself and prayed for his friends, he received healing. His possessions were doubled and he sired ten more children.

> *Then Job answered the Lord, and said, I know that thou canst do every thing, and that no thought can be withholden from thee.*
>
> **—Job 42:1–2 KJV**

(God can read our thoughts; Satan cannot. Satan only hears what we speak and uses our own words against us.) Job admits his lack of knowledge:

> *Who is he that hideth counsel without knowledge? therefore have I uttered that I understood not; things too wonderful for me, which I knew not . . . I have heard of thee by the hearing of the ear: but now mine eye seeth thee. Wherefore I abhor myself, and repent in dust and ashes . . . And the Lord turned the captivity of Job, when he prayed for his friends: also the Lord gave Job twice as much as he had before.*
>
> **—Job 42:3, 5–6, 10 KJV**

Job had an excuse for not knowing the truth about God's character; but what is our excuse? Is it because we haven't studied God's Word through the enlightenment of the Holy Spirit? Have we been indoctrinated by a confused interpretation of the Scriptures, passed down to us by man, without even questioning it? My hope is that this book's message will help bridge the gap between our understanding of God and His true nature.

CHAPTER 9
THE DARKNESS IS UNVEILED

What was the veil spoken of in 2 Corinthians 3:11-16?

> *For if that which is done away was glorious, much more that which remaineth is glorious. Seeing then that we have such hope, we use great plainness of speech: And not as Moses, which put a vail over his face, that the children of Israel could not stedfastly look to the end of that which is abolished: But their minds were blinded: for until this day remaineth the same vail untaken away in the reading of the old testament; which vail is done away in Christ. But even unto this day, when Moses is read, the vail is upon their heart. Nevertheless when it shall turn to the Lord, the vail shall be taken away.*
>
> **—2 Corinthians 3:11–16 KJV**

What was the Old Testament veiled in? I believe it was a blindness that cloaked ancient minds, keeping them from the truth of the God's character.

After Adam fell, the Spirit of God was no longer joined to man's spirit. So their understanding of God was not clear. They couldn't comprehend the difference between God and the law of sin and death. That it is the law which judges, condemns, and punishes. Jesus came with the truth and light that unveiled that darkness. He not only brought the truth about God, He exposed our real enemy—Satan.

It is interesting that there is little written in the Old Testament about Satan. For the most part, he remained hidden.

The following verse in Isaiah has a prophetic double meaning and contains a word of knowledge about Satan:

> *For thou hast trusted in thy wickedness: thou hast said, None seeth me. Thy wisdom and thy knowledge, it hath perverted thee; and thou hast said in thine heart, I am, and none else beside me.*
>
> **—Isaiah 47:10 KJV**

Satan wants to stay hidden so all will blame God and he can do his dirty work—kill, steal, and destroy—uninterrupted. Moses, David, and the other authors of the Old Testament hardly mentioned Satan; they had very little knowledge of him. The word Lucifer is only found one time in the whole King James Bible:

> *How art thou fallen from heaven, O Lucifer, son of the morning! how art thou cut down to*

> *the ground, which didst weaken the nations! For thou hast said in thine heart, I will ascend into heaven, I will exalt my throne above the stars of God: I will sit also upon the mount of the congregation, in the sides of the north.*
>
> **—Isaiah 14:12–13 KJV**

The word Satan is only mentioned eighteen times in the King James Old Testament, of which fourteen of those are in the Book of Job, in the conversation between Satan and God. The Hebrew word for Satan in these eighteen verses is:

Strong's Lexicon / satan / Hebrew #7854: satan saw-tawn' from 7853; an opponent; especially (with the article prefixed) Satan, the arch-enemy of good:–adversary, Satan, withstand.

Strong's Lexicon / Hebrew #7853: satan saw-tan' a primitive root; to attack, (figuratively) accuse:–(be an) adversary, resist.

The word devil is not even found in the King James Old Testament at all, and the word devils is found only four times. All are speaking about people giving sacrifices, sometimes even their children, to pagan gods or devils:

> *Yea, they sacrificed their sons and their daughters unto devils, and shed innocent blood, even the blood of their sons and of their daughters, whom they sacrificed unto the idols of Canaan: and the land was*

polluted with blood.

—Psalm 106:37–38 KJV

So you can see how very few times Satan was even mentioned by the authors of the Old Testament. Satan still tries to hide himself so his work will be uninterrupted. He likes to hide himself and his deceptions. And he loves it when God gets the blame for his evil.

I think it grieves God that our enemy is left out of most sermons throughout American pulpits. How can the church resist and rebuke Satan's lies and temptations if they don't learn what Jesus taught? I realize there are some pastors and teachers who teach God is good most of the time; but when it comes to explaining an unchanging God from Genesis to Revelation, they can't seem to do it. They teach that God loved mankind so much that He came out from Himself and made a human body to sacrifice unto Himself. This is a confused message and I'm afraid it's caused people to turn away from Christianity.

Let's look again at part of Paul's letter to the Corinthians about this veil of darkness:

> *For if that which is done away was glorious, much more that which remaineth is glorious. Seeing then that we have such hope, we use great plainness of speech: and not as Moses, which put a vail over his face, that the children of Israel could not stedfastly look to the end of that which is abolished:*

> *but their minds were blinded: for until this day remaineth the same vail untaken away in the reading of the old testament; which vail is done away in Christ. But even unto this day, when Moses is read, the vail is upon their heart. Nevertheless when it shall turn to the Lord, the vail shall be taken away.*
> **—2 Corinthians 3:11–16 KJV**

What are these verses talking about? Second Corinthians 3:14 is the key verse in this excerpt. It is saying that, even as Paul wrote the words, the same veil still remained on hearts as they read the Old Testament. But Jesus came to show us the Father and unveil the goodness and light of His love. Following is the end of the prayer Jesus prayed in the Garden of Gethsemane, right before He went to Calvary. He is praying for you and me:

> *And I have declared unto them thy name, and will declare it: that the love wherewith thou hast loved me may be in them, and I in them.*
> **—John 17:26 KJV**

Strong's Lexicon / name / Greek #3686: onoma on'-om- ah from a presumed derivative of the base of 1097 (compare 3685); a "name" (literally or figuratively) (authority, character):–called, (+ sur-)name(-d).

Everything we need to know about God is in Jesus Christ. But people don't see it. They still see a God of judgment and wrath. Christianity shares amongst its various denominations the doctrine of salvation through Jesus Christ. And while it's great we got that part right, how have we not seen these truths? Could it be Satan's deception within our own theology infecting the message of Christ?

> *In whom the god of this world hath blinded the minds of them which believe not, lest the light of the glorious gospel of Christ, who is the image of God, should shine unto them.*
>
> **—2 Corinthians 4:4 KJV**

People close their eyes and ears to the truth of the gospel of Jesus:

> *Therefore speak I to them in parables: because they seeing see not; and hearing they hear not, neither do they understand. And in them is fulfilled the prophecy of Esaias, which saith, By hearing ye shall hear, and shall not understand; and seeing ye shall see, and shall not perceive: For this people's heart is waxed gross, and their ears are dull of hearing, and their eyes they have closed; lest at any time they should see with their eyes, and hear with their ears, and should understand with their heart, and should be converted, and I should heal them.*
>
> **—Matthew 13:13–15 KJV**

Some teachers say this is talking about the sinner and the knowledge of salvation. But notice in Matthew 13:17 that "prophets and righteous men" have not understood Christ's teachings about the goodness of God:

> *But blessed are your eyes, for they see: and your ears, for they hear. For verily I say unto you, That many prophets and righteous men have desired to see those things which ye see, and have not seen them; and to hear those things which ye hear, and have not heard them. Hear ye therefore the parable of the sower.*
>
> **—Matthew 13:16–18 KJV**

Amazingly, once the Spirit reveals this to you, you will know the difference between the three laws. You will be able to trace how they each came out of God's original love laws: free will and sowing and reaping.

Have we painted an image of our God as having a huge frowning face looking down on this earth He made? I heard a preacher on TV say once, "God has a big chain on the devil and He loosens or tightens it according to His purpose." Wouldn't that mean God gives sickness and pain, stress, trials, and tribulations to His redeemed to humble them or teach them lessons to make them more righteous? This is not the God that Jesus taught us about!

Have we also painted a loving Jesus, sitting on the right side of God, frantically and desperately trying to get His attention to stop His judgment and wrath on the people? Some teach this is God's righteous judgment.

If we believe God is sovereign and in total control, then we have to believe that God controls all evil. This belief would have the devil working for God if he can't do anything but what God allows him to do.

Have we allowed Satan to deceive us? Have we eaten of his fruit of lies like Adam and Eve did in the Garden? Have our theologians been fooled by Satan's deception, causing a fable in our doctrine that cripples the church and has stolen our miracles?

What do you think about these scriptures?

> *Woe unto them that call evil good, and good evil; that put darkness for light, and light for darkness; that put bitter for sweet, and sweet for bitter!*
>
> **—Isaiah 5:20 KJV**

> *This then is the message which we have heard of him, and declare unto you, that God is light, and in him is no darkness at all.*
>
> **—1 John 1:5 KJV**

> *Be ye not unequally yoked together with unbelievers: for what fellowship hath righteousness with unrighteousness? and what communion hath light with darkness?*
>
> **—2 Corinthians 6:14 KJV**

It's evident to me that part of this darkness (blindness) today is our lack of truth, which has caused our colleges, Bible institutes, and theologians to contribute darkness and evil to a God of love.

As we've said before, the original word from which we get the English translation "judge" has both negative and positive English word meanings:

Strong's Lexicon / judge / Greek #2919: krino kree'-no properly, to distinguish, i.e. decide (mentally or judicially); by implication, to try, condemn, punish:–avenge, conclude, condemn, damn, decree, determine, esteem, judge, go to (sue at the) law, ordain, call in question, sentence to, think.

The only definition of the Hebrew word for judge that we can contribute to God is "to esteem" and "to ordain"— the positive words.

Jesus was a three-part person just as we are, except His Spirit is total deity/God while ours is a human spirit that God joins to at salvation. Deity was housed in a human body with a human soul, mind, will, and emotions. Deity had to come to earth in a human body to do what Adam failed to do. As the Son of man, Jesus came to judge the devil.

Because of the importance of this, it will be mentioned several times in this book. God (deity) does not judge (condemn or punish.) In scripture, Jesus was called the "Son of man" (which spoke of his humanity) and the "Son of God" (which spoke of His deity).

> *For the Father judgeth no man, but hath committed all judgment unto the Son: that all men should honour the Son, even as they honour the Father. He that honoureth not the Son honoureth not the Father which hath sent him. Verily, verily, I say unto you, He that heareth my word, and believeth on him that sent me, hath ever- lasting life, and shall not come into condemnation; but is passed from death unto life . . . And hath given him authority to execute judgment also, because he is the Son of man.*
>
> **—John 5:22–24, 27 KJV**

If God as deity could have judged (condemn and punish), don't you think He would have judged Satan? And if God was really in total control, would He have let Satan split His heaven by the fruit of his lies and convince a third of the angelic host to turn against Him?

Jesus knew that even His own disciples did not understand the truth that He brought to them; it was a mystery to them. But He promised that when He went back to heaven He would send the Comforter—the Spirit of Truth (Holy Spirit)—who would live in us and teach us the deep truths of His Word. Jesus told His disciples the following words:

> *Nevertheless I tell you the truth; It is expedient for you that I go away: for if I go not away, the Comforter will not come unto you; but if I depart, I will send him unto you.*
>
> **—John 16:7 KJV**

Jesus had to go back and sit on the throne of heaven in order to have the ability to come out from Himself and dwell in all of us (at our choice of salvation) in the form of His Spirit, the Holy Spirit.

> *But the anointing which ye have received of him abideth in you, and ye need not that any man teach you: but as the same anointing teacheth you of all things, and is truth, and is no lie, and even as it hath taught you, ye shall abide in him.*
>
> **—1 John 2:27 KJV**

Only the Holy Spirit can bring the light of the gospel to our spirit and soul (mind). There is evidence that some of our professors, theologians, and scholars do not have the Holy Spirit joined to their spirit. How can they teach truth when they doubt truth themselves?

If our interpretation of Scripture causes our doctrine to make the Bible contradict itself, then we have untruth in our doctrine. And if we go by the name "Christian," shouldn't our main message be the same words that Jesus taught? He revealed the Father and exposed Satan, which unveiled the darkness.

CHAPTER 10
THE REST OF THE EASTER STORY

In order to understand this chapter, you must first realize that Jesus Christ was a three-part person, just as we are. We have a spirit and a soul (mind, will, and emotions), which are housed in a body. The difference in Christ and us is that His Spirit is completely deity and our spirit is a human spirit issued to us at conception with a vacant space in the middle to house the Spirit of God. At the moment we receive salvation (accept Jesus Christ as our Savior), a part of God's Spirit comes out from Him and joins to our spirit.

We serve one God who is one Spirit—deity in heaven, deity in Christ, and deity in us called the Holy Spirit or the Spirit of Christ living in us.

Jesus' Spirit was totally God (deity), but because of His human soul, He had free will. He chose to follow God's guidance and speak only God's Words. His Spirit and soul were housed in a human body. He was called the "Son of God" because His Spirit was 100 percent God, and He was called the "Son of man" because His soul and body were 100 percent human.

As the Son of man, Jesus chose to lay down His life to the law of sin and death for us. As the Son of God, His own deity (the Holy Spirit) raised Him up. Jesus said:

> *As the Father knoweth me, even so know I the Father: and I lay down my life for the sheep. And other sheep I have, which are not of this fold: them also I must bring, and they shall hear my voice; and there shall be one fold, and one shepherd. Therefore doth my Father love me, because I lay down my life, that I might take it again. No man taketh it from me, but I lay it down of myself. I have power to lay it down, and I have power to take it again. This commandment have I received of my Father.*
>
> **—John 10:15–18 KJV**

The "other sheep" that Jesus was talking about in the verse above were the Gentiles, meaning all those other than the Jews.

But why was Jesus so discreet about these events of Calvary? Apostle Paul wrote to the Corinthians that none of the princes of this world (demons) knew the mystery (secrets) and hidden wisdom of God or they would not have crucified Christ:

> *But we speak the wisdom of God in a mystery, even the hidden wisdom, which God ordained before the world unto our glory: Which none of the princes of this world knew: for had they*

> *known it, they would not have crucified the Lord of glory . . . But God hath revealed them unto us by his Spirit: for the Spirit searcheth all things, yea, the deep things of God.*
> **—1 Corinthians 2:7–8, 10 KJV**

If Jesus hadn't risen from the dead, there would be no victory over evil, no salvation, no remission for sins, and all of mankind would be eternally lost, forever separated from God. I think Easter is taken far too lightly because most Christians haven't heard the rest of the Easter story. Here is that story:

When Jesus was crucified and died, God the Father (deity in heaven) did not turn His face away from Jesus and forsake Him. Neither did He judge Jesus. Jesus died as a sacrifice to the law of sin and death. His body wasn't sacrificed to God.

When Jesus said, "My God, my God, why hast thou forsaken me?"; according to the original Greek words, He said, "My Deity, my Deity for this intent, leave me."

This is an in-depth word study of the following Bible verse:

> *And about the ninth hour Jesus cried with a loud voice, saying, Eli, Eli, lama sabachthani? that is to say, My God, my God, why hast thou forsaken me?*
> **—Matthew 27:46 KJV**

Love doesn't and cannot forsake, so how do we explain this statement Jesus spoke right before He died? It's really simple; we go to the original Greek words to see what Jesus really said.

Strong's Lexicon / Eli / Greek #2241: eli ay-lee' of Hebrew origin (410 with pronominal suffix); my God:– Eli.

Strong's Lexicon / God / Greek #2316: theos theh'-os of uncertain affinity; a deity, especially (with 3588) the supreme Divinity; figuratively, a magistrate; by Hebraism, very:–X exceeding, God, god(-ly, -ward).

Strong's Lexicon / why / Greek #2444: hinati hin-at-ee' from 2443 and 5101; for what reason ?, i.e. why?:–wherefore, why.

Strong's Lexicon / Greek #2443: hina hin'-ah probably from the same as the former part of 1438 (through the demonstrative idea; compare 3588); in order that (denoting the purpose or the result):–albeit, because, to the intent (that), lest, so as, (so) that, (for) to. Compare 3363.

Strong's Lexicon / forsaken / Greek #1459: egkataleipo eng-kat-al-i'-po from 1722 and 2641; to leave behind in some place, i.e. (in a good sense) let remain over, or (in a bad sense) to desert:–forsake, leave.

According to interpreters of the King James Version Bible, Jesus said, "My God, My God, why hast thou forsaken me?" Along with the original Greek word meanings, we must consider the other words and teachings of Christ about God's character. God is love, and love does not forsake:

> *Beloved, let us love one another: for love is of God; and every one that loveth is born of God, and knoweth God. He that loveth not knoweth not God; for God is love. In this was manifested the love of God toward us, because that God sent his only begotten Son into the world, that we might live through him. Herein is love, not that we loved God, but that he loved us, and sent his Son to be the propitiation for our sins . . . And we have known and believed the love that God hath to us. God is love; and he that dwelleth in love dwelleth in God, and God in him.*
>
> **—1 John 4:7–10, 16 KJV**

The New Testament says that God will never leave us nor forsake us:

> *Let your conversation be without covetousness; and be content with such things as ye have: for he hath said, I will never leave thee, nor forsake thee.*
>
> **—Hebrews 13:5 KJV**

In the Old Testament, God's promise to Joshua:

> *There shall not any man be able to stand before thee all the days of thy life: as I was*

with Moses, so I will be with thee: I will not fail thee, nor forsake thee.

—Joshua 1:5 KJV

When David thought God wasn't hearing him and had forsaken him, God gave him these words during his worship:

I will declare thy name unto my brethren: in the midst of the congregation will I praise thee . . . For he hath not despised nor abhorred the affliction of the afflicted; neither hath he hid his face from him; but when he cried unto him, he heard.

—Psalm 22:22, 24 KJV

Jesus actually said, "My deity, My deity, to this intent, leave me!"

In a very distressed call of pain and agony, Jesus gave His Spirit up into the hands of God the Father.

And when Jesus had cried with a loud voice, he said, Father, into thy hands I commend my spirit: and having said thus, he gave up the ghost.

—Luke 23:46 KJV

In Matthew:

Jesus, when he had cried again with a loud voice, yielded up the ghost. And, behold, the

> *veil of the temple was rent in twain from the top to the bottom; and the earth did quake, and the rocks rent.*
> **—Matthew 27:50–51 KJV**

Strong's Lexicon / ghost / Greek #1606: ekpneo ek-pneh'-o from 1537 and 4154; to expire:–give up the ghost.

At Calvary, the veil that separated the holy of holies (the place where the priests prayed to God for the people) from the rest of the temple was no longer needed. After Calvary, no longer do we need a high priest to pray to God for us. All people—whosoever—can come to God through Jesus, our high priest. If our prayers are based on the truth of God's Word and not half fable, Jesus can repeat them and instruct and command His angels to operate on our behalf. We don't pray to angels, nor does Jesus. But the angels do hearken to His voice and commands.

> *Bless the Lord, ye his angels, that excel in strength, that do his commandments, hearkening unto the voice of his word.*
> **—Psalm 103:20 KJV**

Physicians who have studied what happens to the body when it is crucified say it is the ultimate of all pain. Jesus knew hanging on that cross without His deity—as man alone—and taking on all the sins of the world would be even more excruciating than the pain of crucifixion. Satan's demons were about to come and take His soul to hell. But He was willing; He laid down His life for all of us. He knew it was the only way to win victory and power over Satan, which was the reason He came.

Jesus owned His own body and willingly gave it for us. As the Son of man, Jesus said, "I lay down my life." As the Son of God, He told His disciples. "I have the power, given by the Father, to take it up again."

> *I am the good shepherd: the good shepherd giveth his life for the sheep . . . As the Father knoweth me, even so know I the Father: and I lay down my life for the sheep . . . Therefore doth my Father love me, because I lay down my life, that I might take it again. No man taketh it from me, but I lay it down of myself. I have power to lay it down, and I have power to take it again. This commandment have I received of my Father.*
> **—John 10:11, 15, 17–18 KJV**

When Jesus pushed deity away and took on the sins of the world, He put Himself under the law of sin and death. This gave Satan and his demonic spirits (fallen angels) the opportunity to take His soul (mind) into their domain where the spirits and souls of those who died from Adam and Eve all the way to Calvary were held captive, both in Abraham's bosom and in hell.

In the Old Testament, David prophesied about Jesus being lower than the angels, and about God visiting Him in captivity, joining back to Him, and crowning Him with glory and honor (at His resurrection).

> *What is man, that thou art mindful of him? and the son of man, that thou visitest him? For thou hast made him a little lower than the angels, and hast crowned him with glory and honour.*
> **—Psalm 8:4–5 KJV**

In the New Testament, we find the matching scripture for Psalm 8:5; Paul writing about Jesus fulfilling the Old Testament:

> *But we see Jesus, who was made a little lower than the angels for the suffering of death, crowned with glory and honour; that he by the grace of God should taste death for every man.*
> **—Hebrews 2:9 KJV**

I heard a Christian radio question and answer talk show one day. A caller asked the question, "Did Jesus go to the Father in heaven when He died on the cross, or did He descend into hell?" The host's response was so complicated that the average listener still couldn't know the answer at the end of the broadcast. I'm not sure the host knew for sure himself.

Actually, the question could have been answered by simply saying, "Scriptures support both concepts." And this is why:

1. Jesus' Spirit (deity) went to heaven first, but only for a short time.

   And Jesus said unto him, Verily I say unto thee, Today shalt thou be with me in paradise. And it was about the sixth hour, and there was a darkness over all the earth until the ninth hour. And the sun was darkened, and the veil of the temple was rent in the midst. And when Jesus had cried with a loud voice, he said, Father, into thy hands I commend my spirit: and having said thus, he gave up the ghost.

   —Luke 23:43–46 KJV

   And the graves were opened; and many bodies of the saints which slept arose, And came out of the graves after his resurrection, and went into the holy city, and appeared unto many. Now when the centurion, and they that were with him, watching Jesus, saw the earthquake, and those things that were done, they feared greatly, saying, Truly this was the Son of God.

   —Matthew 27:52–54 KJV

2. When Jesus took on the sins of all mankind on that cross, He allowed Satan's demons to take His soul into hell.

Paul writes to the Ephesians and speaks about Jesus first descending into the lower parts of the earth, and then ascending up far above the heavens, leading those in captivity captive (with him) and giving gifts unto men (the promise of salvation, the Holy Spirit joining to their spirits).

> *(Now that he ascended, what is it but that he also descended first into the lower parts of the earth? He that descended is the same also that ascended up far above all heavens, that he might fill all things.)*
>
> **—Ephesians 4:9–10 KJV**

"Fill all things" simply means fulfilling all the scriptures pertaining to Calvary, from the Crucifixion to the Resurrection.

Jesus fulfilled each prophesy about the Messiah. When He ascended out of hell, He led captivity captive. This was first prophesied in the Old Testament:

> *Thou hast ascended on high, thou hast led captivity captive: thou hast received gifts for men; yea, for the rebellious also, that the Lord God might dwell among them.*
>
> **—Psalm 68:18 KJV**

And then recorded in Ephesians:

> *But unto every one of us is given grace according to the measure of the gift of Christ. Wherefore he saith, When he ascended up on high, he led captivity captive, and gave gifts unto men.*
>
> **—Ephesians 4:7–8 KJV**

In the Old Testament, David prophesied about Jesus' soul descending into hell. Jesus found Himself in the scriptures and knew that God the Father would not leave His soul in hell.

> *Therefore my heart is glad, and my glory rejoiceth: my flesh also shall rest in hope. For thou wilt not leave my soul in hell; neither wilt thou suffer thine Holy One to see corruption. Thou wilt shew me the path of life: in thy presence is fulness of joy; at thy right hand there are pleasures for evermore.*
>
> **—Psalm 16:9–11 KJV**

And the Book of Acts records Peter preaching on the prophecies of David in Psalms being fulfilled by Jesus.

> *For David speaketh concerning him, I foresaw the Lord always before my face, for he is on my right hand, that I should not be moved . . . He seeing this before spake of the resurrection of Christ, that his soul was not left in hell, neither his flesh did see corruption. This Jesus hath God raised up, whereof we all are witnesses.*
>
> **—Acts 2:25, 31–32 KJV**

Satan thought he had captured Jesus the Son of God and nullified redemption for all mankind. But he got the shock of his life when the Holy Spirit burst through the corridors of hell and joined back to Jesus. Satan didn't have a clue as to the magnitude of the event that was about to take place in hell while Jesus' body lay in the tomb.

And that's not all! The greatest war in heaven was about to take place as well. No longer would Satan and his fallen angels traffic in and out of heaven, accusing people to God day and night, just as Satan did of Job.

Jesus said:

> *Now is the judgment of this world: now shall the prince of this world be cast out. And I, if I be lifted up from the earth, will draw all men unto me.*
> **—John 12:31–32 KJV**

Jesus could rejoice in the hope of the Holy Spirit joining back to Him and raising Him up in the fullness of victory and joy at His resurrection. Later, at the right hand of God, Jesus was promised pleasures forevermore, crowned King of kings and Lord of lords!

Luke, the author of Acts, teaches from Psalm 16:11:

> *Wherefore he saith also in another psalm, Thou shalt not suffer thine Holy One to see corruption. For David, after he had served his own generation by the will of God, fell on sleep, and was laid unto his fathers, and saw corruption.*
> **—Acts 13:35–36 KJV**

Luke is simply saying that David wasn't talking about himself in Psalm 16:11 because he died and was not raised from the dead, so his flesh (body) did see corruption. It is evident then that David was prophesying about Jesus, the coming Messiah, who would be raised from the dead and not see corruption.

> *But he, whom God raised again, saw no corruption. Be it known unto you therefore, men and brethren, that through this man is preached unto you the forgiveness of sins: And by him all that believe are justified from all things, from which ye could not be justified by the law of Moses.*
>
> **—Acts 13:37–39 KJV**

As we studied the scriptures in chapter 5, "What Is the Mosaic Law?", we learned that the Mosaic Law did not save for all eternity; it only protected the people from the law of sin and death or simply from having to reap their own sin during their life on earth. So who were the spirits in prison that Jesus preached to and set free from captivity? When did these people repent and believe on Christ for eternal life?

Since it is the knowledge of God that makes mankind accountable, all those who died before Jesus came with the truth about God were not accountable. They were not accountable until they heard Jesus preach in hell.

In the Catholic faith, this belief is called the "Harrowing of Hell." The Catholic Encyclopedia explains it like this:

This is the Old English and Middle English term for the triumphant descent of Christ into Hell (or Hades) between the time of His Crucifixion and His Resurrection, when, according to Christian belief, He brought Salvation to the souls held captive there since the beginning of the world. According to the "New English Dictionary" the word Harrowing in the above connection first occurs in Aelfries homil, about A.D. 1000.[1]

God had given the Hebrew people the gift of the Mosaic Law for a cloak (covering) or protection from the law of sin and death so they wouldn't have to reap their sin. Jesus said:

> *If I had not come and spoken unto them, they had not had sin: but now they have no cloke for their sin.*
> **—John 15:22 JKV**

Peter, a disciple and eyewitness of Jesus Christ, tells us about Jesus suffering for our sins, being put to death in the flesh, quickened by the Spirit, and preaching to the spirits held in prison.

> *For Christ also hath once suffered for sins, the just for the unjust, that he might bring us to God, being put to death in the flesh, but quickened by the Spirit: By which also he*

> *went and preached unto the spirits in prison; Which sometime were disobedient, when once the long-suffering of God waited in the days of Noah, while the ark was a preparing, wherein few, that is, eight souls were saved by water.*
>
> **—1 Peter 3:18–20 KJV**

The above verses reveal that after the crucifixion Jesus preached to the souls who died in the Flood. These folks were some of the most sinful people who ever lived. They were not on the side called Abraham's bosom. Some teachers believe that Jesus only preached to those in Abraham's bosom; the Hebrews who kept the laws of Moses. But according to Scripture, even the most evil heard Jesus.

The following verses say that all of the Hebrews who died in the wilderness tasted of the same spiritual meat and drank of that spiritual Rock that followed after them, which was Christ Jesus.

> *Moreover, brethren, I would not that ye should be ignorant, how that all our fathers were under the cloud, And all passed through the sea; and were all baptized unto Moses in the cloud and in the sea; And did all eat the same spiritual meat; And did all drink the same spiritual drink: for they drank of that spiritual Rock that followed them: and that Rock was Christ.*
>
> **—1 Corinthians 10:1–4 KJV**

These two groups of people (those who died in the days of Noah and the Hebrews who died in the wilderness) were mentioned as examples. But it stands to reason by the Scriptures that Jesus also preached the knowledge of God to the vast number of others who died from Adam to Calvary. It's not God's will that any would perish, because God has no respect of persons. God does not show favoritism:

> *For there is no respect of persons with God.*
> **—Romans 2:11 KJV**

> *The Lord is not slack concerning his promise, as some men count slackness; but is longsuffering to us-ward, not willing that any should perish, but that all should come to repentance.*
> **—2 Peter 3:9 KJV**

As I pondered these scriptures about Jesus descending before He ascended, the following reenactment developed in my mind. This is my version of the account that happened when Jesus visited all the souls who died before His death:

About the time that Satan was rejoicing at the thought that they had Jesus held captive in hell forever and had stopped the whole plan of God's redemption for mankind, he got the shock of his life! Deity God, the Holy Spirit, burst through the corridors of hell and joined back to Jesus.

Jesus fought the demonic angels with the two-edged sword of the Spirit (God's Word). I can only imagine His eyes were like fire and His voice rumbled in power and authority as He spoke the pure truth to Lucifer. After all, the deity in Him was the Word of God who spoke the very existence (creation) of Lucifer. Lucifer had turned God's beautiful law of love, the law of free will and sowing and reaping, into the law of sin and death.

All eyes were on Jesus and by this time all those in Abraham's bosom knew that their Messiah, whom Moses had promised, had come into their midst. I'm sure Moses, Abraham, and the other great prophets of old came forward immediately to praise and honor their Messiah.

Jesus preaches the pure Word of God to all of them and first quotes the prophecies of old that were spoken of Him. I imagine He started with Moses' writings in Genesis 3:15, the prophecy about Jesus bruising the serpent's (Satan's) head at Calvary:

> *And I will put enmity between thee and the woman, and between thy seed and her seed; it shall bruise thy head, and thou shalt bruise his heel.*
>
> **—Genesis 3:15 KJV**

I can hear Jesus quoting these verses but in first person: "I was wounded for your transgressions, I was bruised for your iniquities and the chastisement of your peace was upon me. And with My stripes you are healed!"

> *But he was wounded for our transgressions, he was bruised for our iniquities: the chastisement of our peace was upon him; and with his stripes we are healed. All we like sheep have gone astray; we have turned every one to his own way; and the Lord hath laid on him the iniquity of us all. He was oppressed, and he was afflicted, yet he opened not his mouth: he is brought as a lamb to the slaughter, and as a sheep before her shearers is dumb, so he openeth not his mouth. He was taken from prison and from judgment: and who shall declare his generation? for he was cut off out of the land of the living: for the transgression of my people was he stricken. And he made his grave with the wicked, and with the rich in his death; because he had done no violence, neither was any deceit in his mouth.*
>
> **—Isaiah 53:5–9 KJV**

Then He preached the truth that He came to reveal about Himself being always with God, for He was God's Word made flesh and walked among men to reveal the truth about God and defeat Satan. He offered redemption for the whole human race; all who would receive Him.

I can hear Him continue:

> *This is that bread which came down from heaven: not as your fathers did eat manna, and are dead: he that eateth of this bread*

shall live for ever.

—John 6:58 KJV

I believe Jesus quoted part of John 1 in first person with excitement, power, and anointing so that no one would be left questioning: "In the beginning I was the Word of God that was with God and was God and all things were made by Me, and without Me nothing was made! In Me is Life and this life is the light of men! This Light shined in darkness, but darkness didn't comprehend it. I was in the world and the world was made by Me, and the world knew Me not! But as many as receive Me, I give power to become the sons and daughters of God."

> *In the beginning was the Word, and the Word was with God, and the Word was God. The same was in the beginning with God. All things were made by him; and without him was not any thing made that was made. In him was life; and the life was the light of men. And the light shineth in darkness; and the darkness comprehended it not.*
>
> **—John 1:1–5 KJV**

> *He was in the world, and the world was made by him, and the world knew him not. He came unto his own, and his own received him not. But as many as received him, to them gave he power to become the sons of God, even to them that believe on his name.*
>
> **—John 1:10–12 KJV**

I imagine Jesus went on to say, "I am here to reveal the truth about God to you. God is love, He judges no man and He loves you so much that He came to this earth in My human body to judge Satan and redeem man. I also chose to give My body as the once and for all sacrifice for the sins of the world; and your sins and iniquities I will remember no more!"

> *He that loveth not knoweth not God; for God is love. In this was manifested the love of God toward us, because that God sent his only begotten Son into the world, that we might live through him. Herein is love, not that we loved God, but that he loved us, and sent his Son to be the propitiation for our sins.*
>
> **—1 John 4:8–10 KJV**

> *And as Moses lifted up the serpent in the wilderness, even so must the Son of man be lifted up: that whosoever believeth in him should not perish, but have eternal life. For God so loved the world, that he gave his only begotten Son, that whosoever believeth in him should not perish, but have everlasting life. For God sent not his Son into the world to condemn the world; but that the world through him might be saved.*
>
> **—John 3:14–17 KJV**

> *For it is not possible that the blood of bulls and of goats should take away sins. Wherefore*

when he cometh into the world, he saith, Sacrifice and offering thou wouldest not, but a body hast thou prepared me: In burnt offerings and sacrifices for sin thou hast had no pleasure . . . Then said he, Lo, I come to do thy will, O God. He taketh away the first, that he may establish the second. By the which will we are sanctified through the offering of the body of Jesus Christ once for all . . . But this man, after he had offered one sacrifice for sins for ever, sat down on the right hand of God; From henceforth expecting till his enemies be made his footstool. For by one offering he hath perfected for ever them that are sanctified . . . And their sins and iniquities will I remember no more. Now where remission of these is, there is no more offering for sin. Having therefore, brethren, boldness to enter into the holiest by the blood of Jesus, By a new and living way, which he hath consecrated for us, through the veil, that is to say, his flesh; And having an high priest over the house of God.

—Hebrews 10:4–6, 9–10, 12–14, 17–21 KJV

As those in Abraham's bosom (Hebrews who kept the Mosaic Law) worshiped and accepted their Messiah, I believe Jesus led them all over to the crowd that no man could number, those in Hades who rejected God: everyone from Adam and Eve to those who died in Noah's flood to those up to Judas who betrayed Him. And He preached to them: "You don't have to reap your own sins in this place forever. It is now finished; I have paid the ultimate price; the once and for all sacrifice on the Cross of Calvary for the sins of the whole world! And whosoever believes on Me shall have everlasting life in paradise with God! I am the only door to heaven; I am the way, the truth, and the life, and no one gets to the Father except by Me!"

I can imagine Judas throwing himself down at Jesus' feet weeping from the moment He started preaching. After quoting many Old Testament prophecies about Himself, plus His own teachings, I can see Jesus reaching down and lifting Judas up, holding him in His arms as He spoke to him: "Judas, my disciple, I love you and I forgave you the moment Satan used you. I forgave you the moment you betrayed Me. I prayed for you as I prayed for the Roman soldiers and all who hurt and rejected Me, 'Father forgive them, for they know not what they do!'" I know everyone there bowed and worshiped the King of kings and Lord of lords! About that time, the power of the Spirit of God filled that place and the war was on! Jesus did what He had to do.

WHEN DID HELL GET ITS FLAMES?

It is believed that hell actually got its flames at Calvary as the fiery breath of Jesus blew on it as He fulfilled prophesy and looked back one last time before resurrecting in triumph! The day of the Lord's vengeance was Calvary and the day of Resurrection.

It is my belief that the following verses in Isaiah are a prophecy of Jesus fighting evil in hell and leaving it a burning pitch of fire and brimstone.

> *And the Lord shall cause his glorious voice to be heard, and shall shew the lighting down of his arm, with the indignation of his anger, and with the flame of a devouring fire, with scattering, and tempest, and hailstones. For through the voice of the Lord shall the Assyrian be beaten down, which smote with a rod. And in every place where the grounded staff shall pass, which the Lord shall lay upon him, it shall be with tabrets and harps: and in battles of shaking will he fight with it. For Tophet is ordained of old; yea, for the king it is prepared; he hath made it deep and large: the pile thereof is fire and much wood; the breath of the Lord, like a stream of brimstone, doth kindle it.*
>
> **—Isaiah 30:30–33 KJV**

> *For it is the day of the Lord's vengeance, and the year of recompences for the controversy of Zion. And the streams thereof shall be turned into pitch, and the dust thereof into brimstone, and the land thereof shall become burning pitch. It shall not be quenched night nor day; the smoke thereof shall go up for ever: from generation to generation it shall lie waste; none shall pass through it for ever and ever.*
>
> **—Isaiah 34:8–10 KJV**

> *Then shall he say also unto them on the left hand, Depart from me, ye cursed, into everlasting fire, prepared for the devil and his angels.*
>
> **—Matthew 25:41 KJV**

He locked up so many demons when He cleared the doors and burst forth into resurrection and victory, honor and glory! Praise the Lord our Savior and our King forever more!

My mind can't imagine the magnitude of the excitement when all of heaven stood at attention as Jesus entered clothed in glory, honor, and power, leading this great number of souls robed in white up to the throne! I know the sounds of heaven's orchestra and choirs rang out more beautifully than ever before. This was the greatest celebration, praise and worship, and awe of the glory of God that heaven had ever experienced.

I believe all the angels and redeemed souls fell on their face and worshiped God. This really must have been something because we know the angels rejoice in heaven when just one soul comes into the redemption (salvation) of Christ!

> *Likewise, I say unto you, there is joy in the presence of the angels of God over one sinner that repenteth.*
>
> **—Luke 15:10 KJV**

At the beginning of John's great vision given by Jesus and an angel assisting Him, Jesus said:

> *I am Alpha and Omega, the beginning and the ending, saith the Lord, which is, and which was, and which is to come, the Almighty . . . I am he that liveth, and was dead; and behold, I am alive for evermore, Amen; and have the keys of hell and of death.*
>
> **—Revelation 1:8, 18 KJV**

The events that happened in the spiritual realm at the time of the crucifixion and the three days that followed are enormously important to the human race. Even though Jesus could have accomplished all He did the first day He descended, it took three days before He resurrected.

CHAPTER 11
WHEN WAS THE WAR IN HEAVEN?

Biblical scholars have taught that God kicked Lucifer and his followers (one third of the angels) out of heaven before the creation of Adam and Eve. But if this were the case, wouldn't the story of Job be disannulled? In the Book of Job, Satan was in God's face, accusing Job. Jesus said the Father judges no man, so God the Father did not judge Lucifer and the other rebellious angels or kick them out of heaven before Adam and Eve.

Later in this chapter you will see in Scripture when Jesus, Michael and the other ark angels kicked Lucifer and the fallen angels out of Heaven once and for all; never to accuse the brethren again before God.

By now you recognize that *John 5:22* is a key scripture describing the character of Deity, as well as revealing that one of the reasons Jesus came was to judge Lucifer and the fallen angels, which He did at Calvary and in the Resurrection. It is important to know that Jesus was given "all power" after the Resurrection, which enabled him to clean out Heaven. This battle, I think, took place on Resurrection Day and I am calling it *The War in Heaven*.

This war in Heaven was spoken about in prophecy several times in the Scriptures before it actually happened. Throughout Scripture there were many things spoken of in prophesy that were not, but were spoken of as though they were. Words of prophesy are kind of like words of faith spoken about an incident before it happens:

> *Now faith is the substance of things hoped for, the evidence of things not seen.*
> **—Hebrews 11:1 KJV**

Abraham's wife Sarah believed God in her spirit and mind. Esteeming God faithful, she conceived and had the miracle of a child in her old age.

> *Through faith also Sara herself received strength to conceive seed, and was delivered of a child when she was past age, because she judged him faithful who had promised.*
> **—Hebrews 11:11 KJV**

> *And the angels which kept not their first estate, but left their own habitation, he hath reserved in everlasting chains under darkness unto the judgment of the great day.*
> **—Jude 1:6 KJV**

This war in heaven—before it actually happened, when Jesus and the holy angels fought the demonic spirits, won, and threw them out of heaven once and for all—was spoken of in prophecy several times in the Scriptures before it actually happened.

Throughout Scripture there were many things spoken of in prophesy that were not yet, but were spoken of as though they had already happened. Words of prophesy are kind of like words of faith spoken about an incident before it happens.

> *Now faith is the substance of things hoped for, the evidence of things not seen.*
> **—Hebrews 11:1 KJV**

Abraham also hoped and believed against all hope that he would have a child at 100 years old. God called those things that were not as though they were, and Abraham believed him.

> *Therefore it is of faith, that it might be by grace; to the end the promise might be sure to all the seed; not to that only which is of the law, but to that also which is of the faith of Abraham; who is the father of us all, (As it is written, I have made thee a father of many nations,) before him whom he believed, even God, who quickeneth the dead, and calleth those things which be not as though they were. Who against hope believed in hope, that he might become the father of many nations, according to that which was spoken, So shall thy seed be. And being not*

> *weak in faith, he considered not his own body now dead, when he was about an hundred years old, neither yet the deadness of Sara's womb: He staggered not at the promise of God through unbelief; but was strong in faith, giving glory to God; And being fully persuaded that, what he had promised, he was able also to perform.*
>
> **—Romans 4:16–21 KJV**

Jesus said, "I say nothing except what the Father tells me."

> *Believest thou not that I am in the Father, and the Father in me? the words that I speak unto you I speak not of myself: but the Father that dwelleth in me, he doeth the works.*
>
> **—John 14:10 KJV**

Jesus was made a quickening spirit. This means speaking God's will for a future event as prophesy:

> *And so it is written, The first man Adam was made a living soul; the last Adam was made a quickening spirit . . . The first man is of the earth, earthy: the second man is the Lord from heaven.*
>
> **—1 Corinthians 15:45, 47 NIV**

When Jesus was teaching on this earth, He spoke prophesies about the things that were going to happen around Calvary, which had not happened yet:

> *Now is the judgment of this world: now shall the prince of this world be cast out. And I, if I be lifted up [on the cross] from the earth, will draw all men unto me.*
>
> **—John 12:31–32 KJV**

Jesus was with His disciples on the Mount of Olives when He prayed prophetic words about Calvary, which of course had not happened yet:

> *I have glorified thee on the earth: I have finished the work which thou gavest me to do. And now, O Father, glorify thou me with thine own self with the glory which I had with thee before the world was.*
>
> **—John 17:4–5 KJV**

His purpose on the earth wasn't finished yet because He still had to hang on the cross. And He wasn't glorified until He arose from the dead. At His resurrection, He was crowned with glory and honor and given all power in heaven and earth.

> *Thou madest him a little lower than the angels; thou crownedst him with glory and honour, and didst set him over the works of thy hands . . . But we see Jesus, who was made a little lower than the angels for the suf- fering of death, crowned with glory and honour; that he by the grace of God should taste death for every man.*
>
> **—Hebrews 2:7, 9 KJV**

This was also prophesied about Jesus in the Old Testament:

> *For thou hast made him a little lower than the angels, and hast crowned him with glory and honour. Thou madest him to have dominion over the works of thy hands; thou hast put all things under his feet.*
>
> **—Psalm 8:5–6 KJV**

At His resurrection, Jesus received the power He was prophesied to receive:

> *And Jesus came and spake unto them, saying, All power is given unto me in heaven and in earth.*
>
> **—Matthew 28:18 KJV**

Jesus told Mary Magdalene, the first to see Him after his resurrection, not to touch Him yet:

> *Jesus saith unto her, Touch me not; for I am not yet ascended to my Father: but go to my brethren, and say unto them, I ascend unto my Father, and your Father; and to my God, and your God.*
>
> **—John 20:17 KJV**

After Jesus arose in power, what was so important for Him to do first in heaven, before He came back and stayed forty days on this earth before His final ascension?

It is my belief that Jesus orchestrated this great war in

heaven on the day of His Resurrection. We just covered in chapter 10, "The Rest of the Easter Story," what really happened to Jesus' spirit and soul while His body lay in the tomb until He arose.

I believe Jesus chained up some demonic spirits, as He cleared the way for those spirits from Adam and Eve up to those who died before Calvary to come up with Him.

> *And the angels which kept not their first estate, but left their own habitation, he hath reserved in everlasting chains under darkness unto the judgment of the great day.*
> **—Jude 1:6 KJV**

As Jesus left hell, His spirit and soul joined His body—which was changed into the first new resurrected body of flesh and bone—in the tomb. Praise God! Jesus won victory over death, hell, and the grave! He is alive!

After appearing to Mary Magdalene and telling her to let His disciples know He had risen and would meet with them later, Jesus took His new victory and authority over evil to heaven to fight a one-day war with the help of Michael and other archangels.

I can imagine Jesus had some very powerful words to say to Lucifer before commanding His holy angels to clean out heaven. After all, the deity in Jesus Christ was the same Word of God (Spirit) that created all the angels, including Lucifer. We serve one God, one deity with one Spirit.

In my mind, Jesus' words to Satan went something like this:

"I was the Word that created you perfect in all your ways, and you remained that way until iniquity was found in you. If I had known your ending, I would never have created you! Every precious stone was your covering; you sparkled with flashing gems, the carbuncle and gold!

"Tabrets, tambourine, and pipes were prepared in you the day you were created! Your music played in worship as you walked in the midst of the stones of fire in the mountain of God!

"Yes, all heaven was perfect!

"I loved you as I loved all the angels! You fully knew the substance of deity is pure love and that deity could not judge. And you thought you could be God and sit on His throne? You were no longer satisfied being the angel I created you to be, so you committed suicide and lay down the habitation I had given you, as if that in itself would make you God.

"My first covenants with the angels and with mankind were free will and sowing and reaping. I created these special laws to operate in love.

"Heaven knew no evil, hate, or envy until you came up with them! You devastated My heaven with your jealousy and deceived my angels with your fruit of lies.

"You turned one-third of my angels totally against Me, convincing them to leave their bodies and becoming spirits like deity! And that wasn't enough for you. With your fruit of lies, you tried to destroy My most precious creation—mankind—which was created for My companionship.

"I walked with Adam and Eve in the Garden, teaching them to judge and resist your lies. When they believed your lie that they 'would not surely die' if they chose to believe you, they put all of earth under your curse, not Mine!

"I had to become man to judge you and die as a sacrifice to the curse of the law of sin and death that you created from My first love law of free will and sowing and reaping!

"Now, meet the Son of man who has been given all power to judge you, prince of this earth!

"It is finished, Lucifer! You are done! And you have trafficked in and out of heaven for the last time! The earth I have given to mankind, but from the Day of Pentecost, they shall receive power from Me. The Holy Ghost, My Spirit, will join to their spirit, and I will give them power over you and all of your power.

"My last day church will arise! You will not hold My people hostage. In the latter reign of My Spirit there is victory over all your evil! I will sit at the right hand of deity until you and all your fallen angels are made My footstool! You are defeated!

"You are filled with violence, and thou hast sinned. Therefore I will cast thee as profane out of the mountain of God. And I will destroy thee, O covering cherub, from the midst of the stones of fire.

"Thy heart was lifted up because of thy beauty. Thou hast corrupted thy wisdom by reason of thy brightness. I will cast thee to the ground! I will lay thee before kings, that they may behold thee! Once decreed, My Word and covenant can never change.

"You created the curse of the law of sin and death when you turned My love law of sowing and reaping upside down! So you must reap your own evil destruction of heaven and earth!" Then, Jesus turned to His army and said, "Michael! Angels! Come quickly!"

Like lightning, Satan and his rebellious angels were thrust out of heaven by the powerful commands of the victorious Jesus Christ! Never again would they accuse mankind or the brethren before God.

This great war is recorded in Revelation chapter 12. We agree with the few Bible scholars who theorize that the Book of Revelation is not in chronological order.

That evening, Jesus was back on earth and appeared to His disciples. All except Thomas:

> *Then the same day at evening, being the first day of the week, when the doors were shut where the disciples were assembled for fear of*

> *the Jews, came Jesus and stood in the midst, and saith unto them, Peace be unto you. And when he had so said, he shewed unto them his hands and his side. Then were the disciples glad, when they saw the Lord ... But Thomas, one of the twelve, called Didymus, was not with them when Jesus came.*
>
> **—John 20:19–20, 24 KJV**

Eight days later, Jesus allowed "doubting Thomas" to touch His nail-scarred hands and pierced side so he would also believe Jesus was the risen Christ:

> *And after eight days again his disciples were within, and Thomas with them: then came Jesus, the doors being shut, and stood in the midst, and said, Peace be unto you. Then saith he to Thomas, Reach hither thy finger, and behold my hands; and reach hither thy hand, and thrust it into my side: and be not faithless, but believing. And Thomas answered and said unto him, My Lord and my God. Jesus saith unto him, Thomas, because thou hast seen me, thou hast believed: blessed are they that have not seen, and yet have believed.*
>
> **—John 20:26–29 KJV**

Lucifer exalted himself above other angels. He was lifted up in pride, envy, and jealousy. He actually wanted God's place. His five "I wills" or desires are evident in the following verses of Isaiah:

> *How art thou fallen from heaven, O Lucifer, son of the morning! how art thou cut down to the ground, which didst weaken the nations! For thou hast said in thine heart, I will ascend into heaven, I will exalt my throne above the stars of God: I will sit also upon the mount of the congregation, in the sides of the north: I will ascend above the heights of the clouds; I will be like the most High.*
>
> **—Isaiah 14:12–14 KJV**

As you have seen throughout this book, Jesus came to fulfill the Old Testament. He taught from it, found Himself in its prophecies, and fulfilled all the scriptures concerning the Messiah.

> *Be sober, be vigilant; because your adversary the devil, as a roaring lion, walketh about, seeking whom he may devour.*
>
> **—1 Peter 5:8 KJV**

Satan is our adversary. He is our enemy. It is his goal to kill, steal, and destroy. It is his desire to take as many to hell with him as he can. The only power Satan has is his lies, which sometimes sound like a roaring lion in our heads. But through the Holy Spirit we have been given power over all the power of the enemy.

And the God in us will come in like a flood and raise up a standard against him!

The original Scriptures were written without punctuation. Often, it makes a huge difference where the commas are placed in our translations. Several Bible scholars think that the comma in the following verse was misplaced. I agree. To make Isaiah 59:19 agree with the rest of the teachings of Jesus, the comma needs to be moved:

> *So shall they fear the name of the Lord from the west, and his glory from the rising of the sun. When the enemy shall come in like a flood, the Spirit of the Lord shall lift up a standard against him.*
>
> **—Isaiah 59:19 KJV**

I believe this verse should be punctuated as follows: "When the enemy shall come in, like a flood the Spirit of the Lord shall lift up a standard against him."

As you can see, a simple move of the comma changes the verse's meaning.

It's up to us to resist the devil and ignite the power of God in us through prayers, backed with faith, that agree with the truth of God's Word. God can't do it for us.

> *Submit yourselves therefore to God. Resist the devil, and he will flee from you. Draw nigh to God, and he will draw nigh to you. Cleanse your hands, ye sinners; and purify your hearts, ye double minded . . . Humble yourselves in the sight of the Lord, and he shall lift you up.*
>
> **—James 4:7–8, 10 KJV**

We must find more truth by the Holy Spirit in the Word of God! The truth of God's Word is our map and guide to the power we need to fulfill God's purpose and usher in the kingdom of God on this earth. The truth and praying this truth can and will bring real revival to this lost generation.

If we can become the army God wants us to be, then we can save this generation! But Satan knows his time of freedom on earth is short. The way I see it, he wants to put off his total destruction in the lake of fire as long as he can, by prolonging the wait for Christ's return. This is why he has tried to destroy God's truth by distorting our Christian doctrine with myths and fables.

When most of the church believes in a God of total control over all events on this earth, good or evil, the church has nothing to do but sit and wait on God to do what He wants to when He wants to. This hinders the last day revival and paralyzes the work of the church, which is called and equipped to make God's enemies His footstool.

Some may say, "I thought that all things were put under Jesus' feet at Calvary." My answer would be that they didn't read the end of Hebrews 2:8 to get the complete intended meaning.

Jesus did clean evil out of heaven. But the earth, God had given to the sons of men. And man gave it to Satan. So the way that evil is overcome on earth is through God's design of His divine partnership with us—His Spirit living in us.

His army on this earth is you and me.

> *Thou madest him a little lower than the angels; thou crownedst him with glory and honour, and didst set him over the works of thy hands: Thou hast put all things in subjection under his feet. For in that he put all in subjection under him, he left nothing that is not put under him. But now we see not yet all things put under him. But we see Jesus, who was made a little lower than the angels for the suffering of death, crowned with glory and honour; that he by the grace of God should taste death for every man.*
>
> **—Hebrews 2:7–9 KJV**

We must always have the proof of God's Word to prove our revelation or interpretation of Scripture. Ezekiel's vision (chapter 28) gives a clear description of Lucifer in heaven before and after he sinned, as well as a prophecy of Jesus triumphing over him (at the Resurrection). It ends with a prophecy of Satan's last destruction in the lake of fire.

> *Moreover the word of the Lord came unto me, saying, Son of man, take up a lamentation upon the king of Tyrus, and say unto him, Thus saith the Lord God; Thou sealest up the sum, full of wisdom, and perfect in beauty. Thou hast been in Eden the garden of God;*

every precious stone was thy covering, the sardius, topaz, and the diamond, the beryl, the onyx, and the jasper, the sapphire, the emerald, and the carbuncle, and gold: the workmanship of thy tabrets and of thy pipes was pre- pared in thee in the day that thou wast created. Thou art the anointed cherub that covereth; and I have set thee so: thou wast upon the holy mountain of God; thou hast walked up and down in the midst of the stones of fire. Thou wast perfect in thy ways from the day that thou wast created, till iniquity was found in thee. By the mul- titude of thy merchandise they have filled the midst of thee with violence, and thou hast sinned: therefore I will cast thee as profane out of the mountain of God: and I will destroy thee, O covering cherub, from the midst of the stones of fire. Thine heart was lifted up because of thy beauty, thou hast corrupted thy wisdom by reason of thy brightness: I will cast thee to the ground, I will lay thee before kings, that they may behold thee. Thou hast defiled thy sanctuaries by the multitude of thine iniqui- ties, by the iniquity of thy traffick; therefore will I bring forth a fire from the midst of thee, it shall devour thee, and I will bring thee to ashes upon the earth in the sight of all them that behold thee.

—Ezekiel 28:11–18 KJV

As you can see both the "I wills" in verses 16 and 17

indicate the future tense. At salvation (resurrection), "I [Jesus] will cast thee out of the mountain of God," and, "I will cast thee to the ground." This Old Testament prophecy was for Jesus, as the Son of man, to fulfill. And He did just that.

The latter part of verse 18 and also verse 19 prophesy of Satan's end defeated by Jesus:

> *Therefore will I bring forth a fire from the midst of thee, it shall devour thee, and I will bring thee to ashes upon the earth in the sight of all them that behold thee. All they that know thee among the people shall be astonished at thee: thou shalt be a terror, and never shalt thou be any more.*
> **—Ezekiel 28:18–19 KJV**

This word traffic is speaking about Satan going to and fro in and out of heaven, accusing mankind to God.

In Revelation chapter 12, John recorded this same event—the war in heaven—as the Holy Spirit showed it to him in a vision. The fact that Revelation 12:8 says that the dragon (Satan) and his angels (demonic spirits) would never be found in heaven again means that this war had to take place after Job's experience. The Book of Job starts with a conversation between God and Satan about Job. Satan went up into the presence of God at different times. The statements: "Sin can't stand in the presence of God," and, "If God came into this church today, we would just keel over dead," can't be right. Was Satan sin? Yes, he was the author of it.

We ask sinners to come as they are to receive Christ. The only way a sinner can get saved is to be drawn by the Spirit of God into repentance. God looks at the sinful heart of mankind and draws us to Him with His merciful grace and bountiful love.

It's obvious through many scriptures that Satan went in and out of heaven as he pleased after he chose to leave his body and become a spirit. When did Lucifer and the fallen angels actually leave their bodies to be spirits like God is a Spirit?

The time is not known, because time as we know it starts at Adam and Eve.

> *God is a Spirit: and they that worship him must worship him in spirit and in truth.*
> **—John 4:24 KJV**

We do know the fallen angels left their first estate (their body that God created) before the creation of mankind. This was like a massive suicide and was the first death.

Satan has no new lies or tricks that he hasn't used before to kill, steal, and destroy. This is the same lie he used at the massive suicide deaths of the Jim Jones occult group.

So when was the war in heaven? When was Satan judged? When was Satan cast out, no more to be found in heaven? As the Son of man, Jesus judged Satan when He first descended into hell. The war was on when Jesus ascended up into heaven after His resurrection and Satan fell like lightning.

> *And there was war in heaven: Michael and his angels fought against the dragon; and the dragon fought and his angels, And prevailed not; neither was their place found any more in heaven. And the great dragon was cast out, that old serpent, called the Devil, and Satan, which deceiveth the whole world: he was cast out into the earth, and his angels were cast out with him.*
>
> **—Revelation 12:7–9 KJV**

People need to see this power and victory of Jesus Christ!

I shared the story of the great war in heaven with my grandson Hunter when he was young. His eyes got big and his face showed so much anticipation and awe as I described the scene to him: "There will never be a laser light show as powerful as this lightning when Jesus, Michael, and the archangels kicked the demonic angels out of heaven—out of the great mountain of God, never to enter again!" Revelation 12:10 records the war:

> *And I heard a loud voice saying in heaven, Now is come salvation, and strength, and the*

> *kingdom of our God, and the power of his Christ: for the accuser of our brethren is cast down, which accused them before our God day and night.*
>
> **—Revelation 12:10 KJV**

The only time the word accuser is used in the King James Bible is in Revelation 12:10.

Strong's Lexicon / accuser / Greek #2723: kategoreo kat-ay-gor-eh'-o from 2725; to be a plaintiff, i.e. to charge with some offence:–accuse, object. From G #2596 and Greek #58 Complainant at law; spec. Satan:- accuser.

Strong's Lexicon / Greek #2725: kategoros kat-ay'-gor-os from 2596 and 58; against one in the assembly, i.e. a complainant at law; specially, Satan:–accuser.

Revelation 12:10 also confirms that this fall happened after Adam and Eve were created when it says "accuser of our brethren." Who were the brethren this "accuser" was accusing if this war took place before Adam and Eve?

At salvation (salvation came with the resurrection of Christ), or when Jesus was given all power in heaven and earth and crowned with glory and honor, He cleaned out the sanctuaries of heaven. Satan and his demons were cast down out of heaven once and for all.

Even though Jesus locked up some demonic spirits

when He came out of hell after His crucifixion, when will the rest be locked up? It is our job; the church or body of Christ from the Day of Pentecost until now should have been fulfilling the scriptures and praying prayers of deliverance, locking them up throughout history. It is by our prayers of faith that the angels excel in strength and bind these evil spirits with chains and fetters of iron and cast them into the pit. Wouldn't this world be a better place to live had the church been more focused on fulfilling this purpose? And I believe Christ would have already come before now.

As mankind filled with the power of the Holy Ghost, God has given us the authority to cast out devils. Jesus gave us this command in His last words here on earth—The Great Commission.

> *Know ye not that we shall judge angels? how much more things that pertain to this life?*
> **—1 Corinthians 6:3 KJV**

> *Verily I say unto you, Whatsoever ye shall bind on earth shall be bound in heaven: and whatsoever ye shall loose on earth shall be loosed in heaven.*
> **—Matthew 18:18 KJV**

> *Let the high praises of God be in their mouth, and a two-edged sword [Word of God] in their hand; To execute vengeance upon the heathen, and punishments upon the people*

> *["heathen" and "people" refer to demonic spirits]; To bind their kings with chains, and their nobles with fetters of iron ["kings" and "nobles" refer to the princes of this earth/ demonic spirits]; To execute upon them the judgment written: this honour have all his saints. Praise ye the Lord.*
> **—Psalm 149:6–9 KJV**

After the return of Christ (called the Rapture), the demonic spirits will be locked up for the thousand year millennial reign. They will only to be loosed for a short time at the end of the thousand year reign to tempt those mortals who were born during the 1,000 years, giving them free choice to choose God and His truth or choose Satan's fruit of lies. This is God's gift of love—His covenants of free will and sowing and reaping.

CHAPTER 12

DO OUR TRANSLATIONS OF THE BIBLE CHANGE SCRIPTURE MEANING?

Is it possible our translations of the Bible have changed the original meaning of scriptures to match the doctrine of a God in total control? The more I study, the more I realize they have done just that. This is perhaps our greatest challenge in trying to interpret the Word.

The New International Version has been the most popular translation used in our churches and Bible colleges. Examine with me some of the scriptures often used in sermons after tragedies like 9/11 and how their meanings are affected by different translations:

> *And fear not them [evil men] which kill the body, but are not able to kill the soul: but rather fear him [Satan] which is able to destroy both soul and body in hell.*
>
> **—Matthew 10:28 KJV**

Who is the "him" that tempts us to sin that we might condemn our soul to hell? Who is it this verse is referring to? It is Satan, of course, for he is the one who kills, steals, and destroys. However, the New International Version says:

> *Do not be afraid of those who kill the body but cannot kill the soul. Rather, be afraid of the One who can destroy both soul and body in hell.*
>
> **—Matthew 10:28 NIV**

In taking the liberty to capitalize the word One (which makes the word mean God), the translators have altered the verse to say that God destroys both soul and body in hell.

Let's continue our comparison as Jesus speaks further:

> *Are not two sparrows sold for a farthing? and one of them shall not fall on the ground without your Father. But the very hairs of your head are all numbered. Fear ye not therefore, ye are of more value than many sparrows.*
>
> **—Matthew 10:29–31 KJV**

As you can see, Jesus is telling us, "Not a single sparrow falls without Him seeing it. If He cares that much for the bird, how much more must He care for you! In fact, He cares so much He even knows the number of hairs on your head."

But the New International Version says:

> *Are not two sparrows sold for a penny? Yet not one of them will fall to the ground apart from the will of your Father. And even the very hairs of your head are all numbered. So don't be afraid; you are worth more than many sparrows.*
> **—Matthew 10:29–31 NIV**

This scripture can now be interpreted to say that God has His will in death! In their translation, they have created a confused scripture.

Here is another example of mistranslation falsely confirming God's all-controlling power. First, let's look at the King James Version:

> *Hear counsel, and receive instruction, that thou mayest be wise in thy latter end. There are many devices in a man's heart; nevertheless the counsel of the Lord, that shall stand.*
> **—Proverbs 19:20–21, KJV**

Strong's Lexicon / devices / Hebrew #4284: machashabah makh-ash-aw-baw' or machashebeth makh-ash-eh'-beth; from 2803; a contrivance, i.e. (concretely) a texture, machine, or (abstractly) intention, plan (whether bad, a plot; or good, advice):–cunning (work), curious work, device(-sed), imagination, invented, means, purpose, thought.

This sounds like God is saying, "Follow my guidance

and advice so that you may grow in wisdom," which suggests we have a choice in the matter, that we can choose not to follow God's instruction. Then He says, "My counsel will stand." In other words, it will not pass away.

Strong's Lexicon / counsel / Hebrew #6098: `etsah ay- tsaw' from 3289; advice; by implication, plan; also prudence:– advice, advisement, counsel(l-(or)), purpose.

God's Word is His counsel and instruction, and it will not pass away:

> *Heaven and earth shall pass away, but my words shall not pass away.*
> **—Matthew 24:35 KJV**

And it's plain to see in the following verse that the instruction in God's Word is meant to correct, nurture, and guide our lives:

> *All scripture is given by inspiration of God, and is profitable for doctrine, for reproof, for correction, for instruction in righteousness.*
> **—2 Timothy 3:16 KJV**

Now, let's again take a look at the original verse from Proverbs to see how its meaning has been changed in the New International Version:

> *Listen to advice and accept discipline, and at the end you will be counted among the wise. Many are the plans in a person's heart, but it*

is the Lord's purpose that prevails.
—Proverbs 19:20–21 NIV

This small modification suggests that the word prevail means that God's will—no matter what we decide for ourselves—will win out over our own; that it will be victorious. This would mean God is in total control. But where does our free choice fit in? There is no room for it within this translation.

That sounds like predestination to me!

Can you see why it is so important when studying the Scriptures to get back to the original message intended? Even the smallest mistranslation can change one's entire theology and their understanding of God's character.

CHAPTER 13

HAVE WE CAUSED PEOPLE TO RUN FROM GOD?

For centuries good people have been held outside church walls by the self-righteous and judgmental attitudes within. That is often still true today.

Many teach that everything that happens in the universe is God's doing, that He either causes it or allows it for His will and purpose.

Growing up, I remember hearing the people in church say, "Well, the devil can't do anything except what God allows him to do." Bless their hearts, these godly folks didn't even understand what they were saying! They were just repeating what they'd heard their pastor say. And their pastor was just repeating what he'd heard at Bible school.

Our Christian message has been that God is a sovereign, omnipotent, supreme ruler—one with limitless power. Many have taught that everything that happens in this universe is God's doing, that He either causes or allows it for His will and purpose. If this were true, it would also stand to reason that the devil can't do anything except what God allows him to do. Therefore, does this mean that whenever Satan steals, kills, and destroys, it's actually God doing it through him?

That's starting to sound like Satan works for God! What a mixed-up doctrine that is! In fact, this belief—one Christians have held as truth for centuries—actually makes the Bible seem to contradict itself; it goes completely against what Jesus taught!

Could this confused belief—part of the foundation of the Christian doctrine—actually be driving some to become agnostic?

Lee Strobel, a journalist who investigated the toughest objections to Christianity, writes in his book *The Case for Faith* about his interviews with many agnostics. The following questions and statements are from that book. They are quotes from agnostics:

Why does a good God allow evil to exist?

He must not be powerful enough to deal with all the evil and injustice in the world since it's still going on.

If He is powerful enough to stop wrongdoing, then He must be evil Himself since He's not doing anything about it.

Is He a bad God, or a God that's not all-powerful?[1]

HAVE WE CAUSED PEOPLE TO RUN FROM GOD?

Why are these complex questions about the problem of evil asked of the Christian religion? Because our Christian teachers on radio and TV and at the pulpit have blatantly said that God is all-powerful, in total control of every event on this earth.

Some have said, "There are no surprises to God," and, "All tragedies in this life are gifts and blessings from God." Many times in the same sermon they'll teach both that God is a God of love who will never leave us and God is a God of judgment and condemnation. With ideas like this, I can see why people are scared of God and want to run from Him.

What would cause a minister to turn agnostic when in their early thirties he and Reverend Billy Graham were close friends and preaching colleagues?

After abandoning journalism for the ministry, Charles Templeton met Graham in 1945, at a Youth for Christ rally. They were roommates and constant companions during an adventurous tour of Europe, alternating in the pulpit as they preached at rallies. Templeton founded a church that soon overflowed its 1200-seat sanctuary. American Magazine said he set a new standard for mass evangelism. But soon doubts began gnawing at Templeton. "My reason had begun to challenge and sometimes to rebut the central beliefs of the Christian faith."[2]

Lee Strobel interviewed Charles Templeton at his home

in a high-rise penthouse in Toronto. Strobel found this ex-preacher and agnostic journalist sick with the Alzheimer's disease he had previously written about in his book *Farewell to God*.

He pointed out the horrors of Alzheimer's disease, describing in gripping detail the way it hideously strips people of their personal identity by rotting their minds and memory.

"How," he demanded, "could a compassionate God allow such a ghastly illness to torture its victims and their loved ones?" The answer, he concluded, is simple: "Alzheimer's would not exist if there were a loving God, and because it does exist, that's one more bit of persuasive evidence that God does not."[3]

Strobel asked if there was one thing in particular that caused him to lose his faith in God. Templeton thought for a moment.

"It was a photograph in Life magazine," he said finally. "It was a picture of a black woman in Northern Africa," he explained. "They were experiencing a devastating drought. And she was holding her dead baby in her arms and looking up to heaven with the most forlorn expression. I looked at it and I thought, 'Is it possible to believe that there is a loving or caring Creator when all this woman needed was rain?' How could a loving God do this to that woman?" he implored. "Who runs the rain? I don't;

you don't. He does—or that's what I thought. But when I saw that photograph, I immediately knew it is not possible for this to happen and for there to be a loving God. There was no way. Who else but a fiend could destroy a baby and virtually kill its mother with agony—when all that was needed was rain? . . . It just became crystal clear to me that it is not possible for an intelligent person to believe there is a deity that loves."[4]

Even now when I read this story in Strobel's book, the tears fall. Have we contributed to people turning agnostic and atheistic? Who told them that God controlled the universe, the weather, the storms, and the droughts?

Bart D. Ehrman is the James A. Gray distinguished Professor of Religious Studies New Testament at the University of North Carolina Chapel Hill and is the author of over twenty books. In his books, he recounts his youthful enthusiasm as a born-again fundamentalist Christian.

His graduate studies, however, eventually convinced him that one ought to acknowledge the contradictions in the biblical manuscripts rather than attempt to harmonize or reconcile discrepancies. He remained a "liberal Christian" for fifteen years and served as youth pastor, director of education, and then as an interim pastor of Princeton Baptist Church. But after struggling with the philosophical problems of evil and suffering, he became an agnostic.

This sounds like attending three Bible Institutes—Moody Bible Institute, Wheaton College, and the Princeton

Theological Seminary—caused him to doubt the Word of God as well as the very existence of God. There's something very wrong with this picture. Isn't the purpose of the Bible institute to train and prepare men and women for the pulpits of America?

After reading his three latest books, it is evident to me that Bart's problem comes from two causes but one source: the fruit of Satan's lies:

1. The fable in modern theology, even more evident in the new translations

2. Misquoting scripture; repeating Satan's fruit of lies (blasphemy)

Like Eve, Ehrman pushed God's Spirit out of his spirit leaving an open door for deception and the influence of Satan's lies.

As we have seen in the Scriptures, there is no way to understand the meaning of God's Word without the Holy Spirit joined to our spirit.

> *But the anointing which ye have received of him abideth in you, and ye need not that any man teach you: but as the same anointing teacheth you of all things, and is truth, and is no lie, and even as it hath taught you, ye shall abide in him.*
>
> **—1 John 2:27 KJV**

If God was who the church says He is—full of judgment,

wrath, and punishment—He would have zapped Ehrman for his lies about Him and His Holy Word. But God doesn't zap or strike anyone down.

Even though the multitude of souls that have been influenced by Bart's teaching I'm sure has tremendously grieved God, His unchanging unconditional love for Bart D. Ehrman has never changed. The truth is, God has knocked on Bart's heart's door ever since he pushed Him out.

In one of Bart's books, he recalls visiting a Christmas program at his wife's church and tears filling his eyes at the thought of deity coming to earth to die for our sins. He threw it off as just human emotion. He also wrote about awakening abruptly out of sleep, sitting straight up in bed in a cold sweat with the thought, "What if I'm wrong?" In a letter I wrote to Ehrman, I expressed that those times were both signs that God was wanting back in his heart.

The college professors, teachers, ministers, and all leaders have a huge influence, not only on us but also on our children and grandchildren. We need to pray for our teachers, that they come into the light and truth of the gospel of Christ.

SO, HAVE WE CAUSED PEOPLE TO RUN FROM GOD?

I heard a radio minister say, "You can have peace of mind when you accept the fact that everything in this universe that takes place is God's plan and doing." This is such a wrong theology! I can't imagine how much it must hurt God's heart for His own children to make these claims. I truly believe there are some missing links in our modern theology which include the lack of the knowledge of God's first covenants—free will and sowing and reaping—and the study of the law of sin and death. Without this knowledge it is impossible to know God's true character.

Is He a God of wrath or a God of love? Does He know all my choices before I make them? Is He one deity or three persons called the Trinity? Just who is God? (For more study on the subject see Book Two: *God Out of the Shadows.*)

CHAPTER 14
WOULD THE REAL GOD PLEASE STAND UP?

Since there are so many different religions growing among America's youth, how can they be turned to the one true God? It will take what it has always taken: signs and wonders and healing miracles, just as it did for Elijah, Moses, even Jesus, and the first church in the Book of Acts.

As a USA Today news article so perfectly put it, America is "still one nation under God . . . But whose God?"[1]

According to the ten-year survey reported in the same USA Today article on December 24, 2001, while Christianity fell by 8 percent, the percentage of growth in these non-Christian religions from 1990–2001 will shock most of us. And even more significant is the fact that the majority of the growth came from our country's youth. The survey showed:

- Muslims up 110 percent—95 percent youth
- Buddhists up 170 percent—95 percent youth
- Hindus up 237 percent—96 percent youth

- Unitarians up 25 percent—97 percent youth
- Wiccans up 1,575 percent—99 percent youth
- No religion or atheist, agnostic, humanist, and secular up 106 percent—6 percent youth.[2]

This survey shows the decline in Christianity and the huge growth pattern of non-Christian religions.

Keep in mind, who and what a person listens to is their source of information and often becomes their belief and personal paradigm. Between media influence, the entertainment industry, and the influx of other religions through immigration, who our young people listen to has changed drastically over the past few generations. But what are even more detrimental to the truth of the Word are the fables and lies that Satan has injected into the story of Christ's redeeming love. This generation needs a major paradigm shift from fables to real truth about God and His love for all mankind.

This survey and the facts it reveals reminds me of the story of Elijah and the prophets of Baal:

The children of Israel were torn between two gods and even doubted the miraculous God of their fathers. They had forgotten all the blessings and miracles God had done for them. They had left their God to worship Baal and found themselves in a three-year drought. Full of confusion, their minds must have at times wondered, "Whose God is the real God?"

Just like Americans are confused about God today, so were the children of Israel. And they too were in bad need of a paradigm shift. It took a visible miracle to show them the real God and turn their hearts back to Him.

Israel's king at the time, Ahab, had failed to acknowledge the Lord and had allowed himself and all Israel to be seduced into Baal worship by his wife Jezebel.

God told His prophet Elijah to go to Ahab and He would send them rain. God wanted to work miracle through Elijah so the children of Israel would believe in Him again.

> *And it came to pass after many days, that the word of the Lord came to Elijah in the third year, saying, Go, shew thyself unto Ahab; and I will send rain upon the earth. And Elijah went to shew himself unto Ahab. And there was a sore famine in Samaria.*
> **—1 Kings 18:1–2 KJV**

Jezebel was killing the prophets of God, trying to stop God's message. A good man named Obadiah hid 100 of these prophets of God to protect them from her hand of murder.

> *For it was so, when Jezebel cut off the prophets of the Lord, that Obadiah took an hundred prophets, and hid them by fifty in a cave, and fed them with bread and water.*
> **—1 Kings 18:4 KJV**

At some point, Ahab told Obadiah to go find springs and brooks of water and grass for the horses and mules to keep them alive in the drought. Elijah was on his way to King Ahab when Obadiah met him:

> *And as Obadiah was in the way, behold, Elijah met him: and he knew him, and fell on his face, and said, Art thou that my lord Elijah? And he answered him, I am: go, tell thy lord, Behold, Elijah is here . . . So Obadiah went to meet Ahab, and told him: and Ahab went to meet Elijah. And it came to pass, when Ahab saw Elijah, that Ahab said unto him, Art thou he that troubleth Israel?*
> **—1 Kings 18:7–8, 16–17 KJV**

It sounds like Ahab was blaming Elijah, this prophet of God, for the drought.

> *And he answered, I have not troubled Israel; but thou, and thy father's house, in that ye have forsaken the commandments of the Lord, and thou hast followed Baalim. Now therefore send, and gather to me all Israel unto mount Carmel, and the prophets of Baal four hundred and fifty, and the prophets of the groves four hundred, which eat at Jezebel's table.*
> **—1 Kings 18:18–19 KJV**

There comes a time that people have to see God's signs and wonders before they will believe. God wanted to use

Elijah in a showdown of His power against Baal. Elijah told Ahab to gather all of Israel and the prophets of Baal upon Mount Carmel where the Canaanites built sanctuaries of pagan weather deities or gods. What an ideal place for a confrontation to show the superiority of the Lord. After all, their weather gods had not sent rain.

The prophet Elijah met the people and spoke with power and confidence because he knew the same God that worked miracles through him before would certainly not let him down this time.

Elijah's shouts rang out over the mountaintop and echoed across the next valley:

> *And Elijah came unto all the people, and said, How long halt ye between two opinions? if the Lord be God, follow him: but if Baal, then follow him. And the people answered him not a word.*
>
> **—1 Kings 18:21 KJV**

Then Elijah said, "Only I remain a prophet of the Lord, but Baal's prophets are 450 men." He gives the instructions, "Let them bring us each a bullock to cut into pieces and lay on our own altars of wood with no fire under it." The instructions were clear and completely fair.

> *And call ye on the name of your gods, and I will call on the name of the Lord: and the God that answereth by fire, let him be God. And*

> *all the people answered and said, It is well spoken. And Elijah said unto the prophets of Baal, Choose you one bullock for yourselves, and dress it first; for ye are many; and call on the name of your gods, but put no fire under. And they took the bullock which was given them, and they dressed it, and called on the name of Baal from morning even until noon, saying, O Baal, hear us. But there was no voice, nor any that answered. And they leaped upon the altar which was made.*
>
> **—1 Kings 18:24–26 KJV**

Elijah told them, "Cry louder, for he is either too busy talking or pursuing other things. Maybe he's on a journey or asleep, and you need to wake him up!"

They cried loudly, but there was still no answer and no fire. So they cut themselves with their own knives. Midday came and went, and the prophets of Baal prophesied until it was time for the evening sacrifice. There had been no voice, no answer, nor any response at all from their pagan gods. Then the echo of Elijah's voice could be heard coming over the mountain. "Come near to me!" Elijah was not arrogant. He just wanted the people to believe in the "living God," who wanted them to have rain.

It is likely the same evil spirits that enforced the curse of the law of sin and death on the earth causing Noah's flood were the ones causing the drought. It would take Elijah's prayers and those of the children of Israel to change the elements and bring rain.

Elijah then built the altar of the Lord with twelve stones representing the twelve tribes of the sons of Jacob. Elijah built the altar in the name of the Lord and made a trench around it that would hold two whole measures of seed. He put the wood in place, cut the bullock in pieces, and laid it on the wood.

His next instructions startled them so greatly that they obeyed—despite the shortage of water. Elijah ordered four barrels full of water to pour on the burnt sacrifice and the wood. They knew it was impossible for water to burn, and Elijah didn't stop with just four barrels:

> *And he said, Do it the second time. And they did it the second time. And he said, Do it the third time. And they did it the third time. And the water ran round about the altar; and he filled the trench also with water.*
> **—1 Kings 18:34–35 KJV**

Twelve big barrels of water were poured onto the entire altar, the sacrifice, and the trenches around the altar. Elijah's confidence and faith were unwavering. He knew that his God would come through.

> *And it came to pass at the time of the offering of the evening sacrifice, that Elijah the prophet came near, and said, Lord God of Abraham, Isaac, and of Israel, let it be known*

> *this day that thou art God in Israel, and that I am thy servant, and that I have done all these things at thy word. Hear me, O Lord, hear me, that this people may know that thou art the Lord God, and that thou hast turned their heart back again. Then the fire of the Lord fell, and consumed the burnt sacrifice, and the wood, and the stones, and the dust, and licked up the water that was in the trench. And when all the people saw it, they fell on their faces: and they said, The Lord, he is the God; the Lord, he is the God.*
>
> —**1 Kings 18:36–39 KJV**

The real God stood up for them that day, and all the children of Israel believed on God once again; all except those prophets of Baal who ate at Jezebel's table.

> *And Elijah said unto them, Take the prophets of Baal; let not one of them escape. And they took them: and Elijah brought them down to the brook Kishon, and slew them there.*
>
> —**1 Kings 18:40 KJV**

You see, the 450 prophets of Baal were possessed with demonic spirits. Who is the god Baal?

Strong's Concordance: Baal: 1. Chief god of the Canaanites.

And when the Prophets of Baal prayed most of the day and got no response from their pagan gods, they started cutting themselves with knives. To me this is evidence that they were possessed with demonic spirits, because Jesus said that the thief or devil steals kills and destroys:

> *The thief cometh not, but for to steal, and to kill, and to destroy: I am come that they might have life, and that they might have it more abundantly.*
>
> **—John 10:10 KJV**

Also, the man with the legion of demons that Jesus cast into the pigs was known to cry aloud or scream while he cut himself with stones:

And always, night and day, he was in the mountains, and in the tombs, crying, and cutting himself with stones. For he (Jesus) said unto him, Come out of the man, *thou* unclean spirit. And he (Jesus) asked him, What *is* thy name? And he answered, saying, My name *is* Legion: for we are many. (Mark 5:5, 8-9)

Before Jesus came, the only way to get rid of the evil possession was to destroy the temple or body that the demonic spirit had possessed. Jesus was the first to cast out a devil and set the captive free.

As we established in chapter 11, "The Rest of the Easter Story," all who died before Calvary were given a chance to choose salvation when Jesus went into hell and preached to all who were held captive. I'm expecting to see these 450 prophets of Baal in heaven.

Then Elijah said to Ahab, "Go eat and drink for there

is a sound of abundance of rain." Did Elijah hear the rain? Had the rain started? No, there was not even a cloud in the sky. He was speaking words of faith because God had told him that if he would go to Ahab, rain would come and stop the drought. Elijah was speaking things that were not as though they were.

Elijah went up to the top of Carmel, and there he knelt down on the ground to pray. He said to his servant, "Go look toward the sea and tell me if you see a rain cloud?"

"There is nothing," the servant said, after returning. Elijah said, "Well, go again and look seven times."

> *And it came to pass at the seventh time, that he said, Behold, there ariseth a little cloud out of the sea, like a man's hand. And he said, Go up, say unto Ahab, Prepare thy chariot, and get thee down, that the rain stop thee not. And it came to pass in the mean while, that the heaven was black with clouds and wind, and there was a great rain. And Ahab rode, and went to Jezreel. And the hand of the Lord was on Elijah; and he girded up his loins, and ran before Ahab to the entrance of Jezreel.*
>
> **—1 Kings 18:44–46 KJV**

By Elijah's obedience and faith, the Lord God did just what He had promised. Their drought turned into rain. How much more should God's miracles work through us today since we have God living inside of us, joined to our spirit (as the Holy Spirit).

Is the Jezebel spirit that entered the Christian church in the Thyatira church age still working today? Is it trying to kill the truth and stop the true message of God? Is America torn between its gods? Is America wondering which one is real, doubting the God of our fathers as Israel did and falling into the worship of pagan gods? God wants to show His great power and love to America and this world. He is ready to stand up through you and me.

I believe it is time for some signs and wonders like the prophets of old experienced. Don't you? I know that the Lord God of Abraham, Isaac, and Jacob—the God of Israel—will not fail us but will be faithful to perform those things He has promised. I want to be an Elijah. How about you? According to the many scriptures in this book, every believer is to be like Elijah with signs and wonders following him.

I'm excited about America's future. I'm excited about our awakening and renewed hunger for the truth of God's Word, which is the key to the last days revival and great harvest of souls.

God gave the Great Commission to all of us who believe. Let us dig deeper in the Word, climb higher in the Spirit, and walk a straighter path that we might see His miraculous signs and wonders performed. It's not "Can we trust God?" but "Can God trust us to do His works?" so that souls are led into His kingdom to everlasting life in eternal heaven. Don't let our worship be carnal and fleshly, but let us worship with a pure heart in Spirit and in truth.

I thank God that we have had the right salvation message. Salvation is the one single most important decision that an individual will ever make in their lifetime. This experience of salvation can take place at any time, day or night, that you call upon the name of the Lord Jesus Christ. The Holy Spirit will draw and beckon all to come to God when His Word is heard or read.

At your whispered prayer, He'll be right there.

> *No man can come to me, except the Father which hath sent me draw him: and I will raise him up at the last day. It is written in the prophets, And they shall be all taught of God. Every man therefore that hath heard, and hath learned of the Father, cometh unto me.*
>
> **—John 6:44–45 KJV**

In verse 45 above, Jesus is saying, "If you hear the gospel, the Spirit of God will draw you and cause you to come to Me." All are welcome, all are loved, because it isn't God's will for any to perish. But each individual has to make his or her own choice because of the free will God gave us.

Jesus is sometimes referred to as the Bread of Life:

> *Then Jesus said unto them, Verily, verily, I say unto you, Moses gave you not that bread from heaven; but my Father giveth you the*

> *true bread from heaven. For the bread of God is he which cometh down from heaven, and giveth life unto the world. Then said they unto him, Lord, evermore give us this bread. And Jesus said unto them, I am the bread of life: he that cometh to me shall never hunger; and he that believeth on me shall never thirst . . . Verily, verily, I say unto you, He that believeth on me hath everlasting life. I am that bread of life. Your fathers did eat manna in the wilderness, and are dead. This is the bread which cometh down from heaven, that a man may eat thereof, and not die. I am the living bread which came down from heaven: if any man eat of this bread, he shall live for ever: and the bread that I will give is my flesh, which I will give for the life of the world.*
>
> **—John 6:32–35, 47–51 KJV**

This includes everyone in this world!

> *This is that bread which came down from heaven: not as your fathers did eat manna, and are dead: he that eateth of this bread shall live for ever . . . It is the spirit that quickeneth; the flesh profiteth nothing: the words that I speak unto you, they are spirit, and they are life.*
>
> **—John 6:58, 63 KJV**

> *Seek ye the Lord while he may be found, call ye upon him while he is near: let the wicked*

> *forsake his way, and the unrighteous man his thoughts: and let him return unto the Lord, and he will have mercy upon him; and to our God, for he will abundantly pardon.*
>
> **—Isaiah 55:6–7 KJV**

> *For God so loved the world, that he gave his only begotten Son, that whosoever believeth in him should not perish, but have everlasting life. For God sent not his Son into the world to condemn the world; but that the world through him might be saved.*
>
> **—John 3:16–17 KJV**

> *But now being made free from sin, and become servants to God, ye have your fruit unto holiness, and the end everlasting life. For the wages of sin is death; but the gift of God is eternal life through Jesus Christ our Lord.*
>
> **—Romans 6:22–23 KJV**

> *Jesus said unto her, I am the resurrection, and the life: he that believeth in me, though he were dead, yet shall he live: and whosoever liveth and believeth in me shall never die. Believest thou this?*
>
> **—John 11:25–26 KJV**

There are three simple steps to have God join to your spirit and give you salvation:

1. Believe that Jesus Christ is the Word of God, that He came out from the Father, that He is the Messiah, and that He arose on the third day with the first glorified body.

2. Repent and confess your sins to Him.

3. Receive, by faith, His free gift of grace, redemption, and salvation

If you don't know Jesus, I invite you to step into a personal relation with God today. God's desire is to stand up in you like He did in Elijah and turn the hearts of mankind to Him. Say this prayer with me to begin your journey as a soldier of God:

Lord, I spiritually lay this fleshly body down in front of the altar of Your mercy seat. Now cleanse me, Lord, from all my sins and all unforgiveness I have toward those who have disappointed me. I give You all the situations in my life that disappointed me, and I forgive everyone who has hurt me. Lord, wash my spirit clean of all the hurts of my past.

Forgive me, Lord, for blaming You and being angry with You for the bad things that have happened in my life. I know now it wasn't You. I'm sorry for the grief that caused You. But Your great, unconditional love for me never changed, and You never stopped knocking at my heart's door. I love You, Lord Jesus, and I receive You into my heart, that You and I might become one in Spirit. Cleanse me daily, moment by moment, as I die daily to my fleshly desires of sin. I will allow Your Spirit to be my Teacher, Counselor, my Comforter, and my Guide. Lord, I receive all that You did for me at Calvary—healing my mind, my body, and my spirit.

Fill me now, Lord, with Your joy and peace that my joy might be full. Point my toes toward the mark of Your high calling for me. I want neither detours nor wavering to the left or to the right.

Lord, teach me and reveal the knowledge of Your Word to me that I might really know You. I will put Your Word in my heart that it might freely flow up out of my spirit like springs of living waters all over me and those around me. Only then can I see those around me through Your eyes of love and understanding and through Your compassion.

Now, let us pray together as Americans for our nation and our future:

Lord, we the people of America repent for being a spiritual sleeping giant and we repent for blaming others for the moral sins of this nation. Lord, You said, "If My people who are called by My name will humble themselves and pray," that You would heal our land. Lord, we do repent for blaming any pain, death, or any tribulation on You. We realize now that this was Satan's deception and that this deception has been holding America back from winning its great harvest of souls.

Forgive us, Lord, and fill us with Your Spirit of love

and power, that we might do Your Great Commission on this land, our homeland. Help us all together—red, yellow, black, and white—become that great nation that our forefathers dreamed of. We pray that Your peace, freedom, love, and truth will reign throughout this world with all people. Amen.

America, arise to the call of God once more so that you may once again be called blessed among nations!

God Bless America!

CHARTS

GOD FREE WILL SOWING AND REAPING

CHART # 1

COVENANT
WORD

FREE WILL

(Deu 30:19 KJV) I call heaven and earth to record this day against you, that I have set before you life and death, blessing and cursing: <u>therefore choose life</u>, that both thou and thy seed may live:

(Josh 24:15 KJV) And if it seem evil unto you to serve the LORD, <u>choose you this day</u> whom ye will serve;

(Rev 22:17 KJV) And the Spirit and the bride say, Come. And let him that heareth say, Come. And let him that is athirst come. And <u>whosoever will, let him</u> take the water of life freely.

SOWING AND REAPING

(Gal 6:7 KJV) Be not deceived; God is not mocked: for <u>whatsoever a man soweth, that shall he also reap.</u>

(Gal 6:8 KJV) For <u>he that soweth</u> to his flesh <u>shall of the flesh reap</u> corruption; but <u>he that soweth</u> to the Spirit shall of the Spirit <u>reap life everlasting.</u>

(Luke 6:31 KJV) And as ye would that men should <u>do to you, do ye also to them</u> likewise.

(1 John 4:19 KJV) <u>We love him, because he first loved us.</u>

(Psa 89:34 KJV) <u>My covenant</u> will I not break, <u>nor alter</u> the thing that is gone out of my lips.

(Heb 6:18 KJV) That <u>by two immutable things,</u> in which it was <u>impossible for God to lie,</u> we might have a strong consolation, who have fled for refuge to lay hold upon the hope set before us: (OATH AND THE PROMISE BASED ON <u>FREE WILL</u> AND <u>SOWING AND REAPING</u>)

(Psa 138:2 KJV) I will worship toward thy holy temple, and praise thy name for thy lovingkindness and for thy truth: <u>for thou hast magnified thy word above all thy name.</u>

(1 Cor 13:5 KJV) (LOVE)- Doth not behave itself unseemly, seeketh not her own, is not easily provoked, <u>thinketh no evil;</u>

(1 John 4:8 KJV) He that loveth not knoweth not God; for <u>God is love.</u>

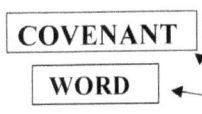

CHARTS

GOD   CHART # 2
FREE WILL
SOWING AND REAPING

[COVENANT]
[WORD]

LOVE

LAW OF THE SPIRIT OF LIFE

(Rom 8:1 KJV) There is therefore now no condemnation to them which are in Christ Jesus, who walk not after the flesh, but after the Spirit.

(Rom 8:2 KJV) For the law of the Spirit of life in Christ Jesus hath made me free from the law of sin and death.

(Gal 6:8 KJV) For he that soweth to his flesh shall of the flesh reap corruption; but he that soweth to the Spirit shall of the Spirit reap life everlasting. (eternal life)

(Titus 1:2 KJV) In hope of eternal life, which God, that cannot lie, promised before the world began;

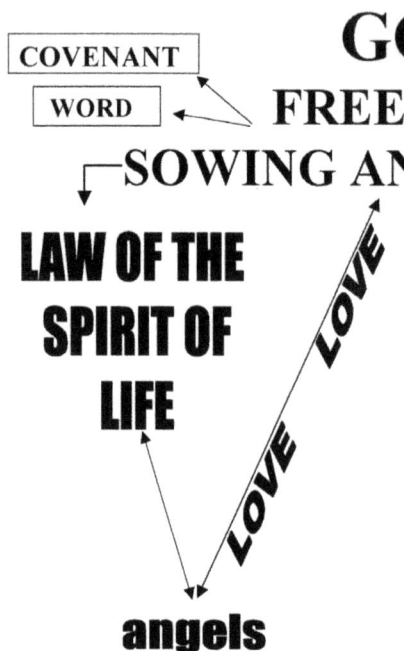

GOD
FREE WILL
SOWING AND REAPING

COVENANT
WORD

LAW OF THE SPIRIT OF LIFE

LOVE LOVE LOVE

angels

CHART # 3

(Heb 1:4 KJV) Being made so much better than the angels, as he hath by inheritance obtained a more excellent name than they.
(Ro 8:17 KJV) And if children, then heirs; heirs of God, and joint-heirs with Christ;
(Heb 1:5 KJV) For unto which of the angels said he at any time, Thou art my Son, this day have I begotten thee? And again, I will be to him a Father, and he shall be to me a Son?
(1 Jo 3:1 KJV) Behold, what manner of love the Father hath bestowed upon us, that we should be called the sons of God; therefore the world knoweth us not, because it knew him not.
(Heb 1:14 KJV) Are they not all ministering spirits, sent forth to minister for them who shall be heirs of salvation?
(Psa 103:20 KJV) Bless the LORD, ye his angels, that excel in strength, that do his commandments, hearkening unto the voice of his word.
(Rom 10:8 KJV) But what saith it? The word is nigh thee, even in thy mouth, and in thy heart: that is, the word of faith, which we preach;
(1 Cor 6:3 KJV) Know ye not that we shall judge angels? how much more things that pertain to this life?

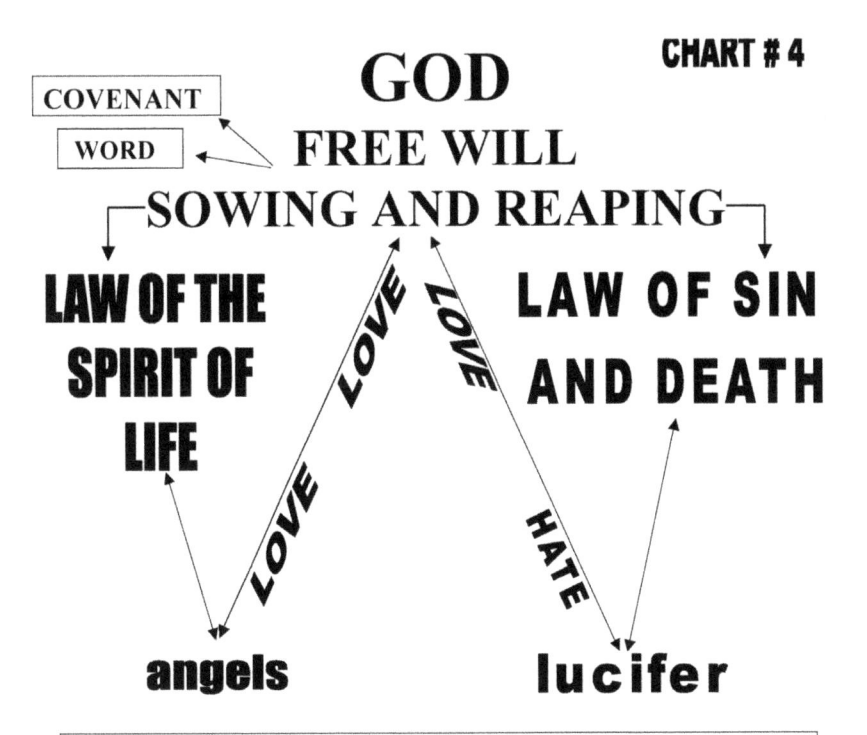

CHARTS

CHART # 4

GOD
FREE WILL
COVENANT
WORD

SOWING AND REAPING

LAW OF THE SPIRIT OF LIFE — LOVE / LOVE / LOVE / LOVE — **LAW OF SIN AND DEATH**

LOVE ↓ angels   HATE ↓ lucifer

(Isa 14:13 KJV) For thou hast said in thine heart, I will ascend into heaven, I will exalt my throne above the stars of God: I will sit also upon the mount of the congregation, in the sides of the north:

(Isa 14:14 KJV) I will ascend above the heights of the clouds; I will be like the most High.

(Ezek 28:15 KJV) <u>Thou wast perfect</u> in thy ways from the day that thou wast created, <u>till iniquity was found in thee</u>.

SIN = (AN ACT OF REBELLION BASED UPON FREE WILL)

(Jude 1:6 KJV) And the <u>angels which kept not their first estate, but left their own habitation,</u>

(Rom 8:2 KJV) For the <u>law of the Spirit of life</u> in Christ Jesus hath made me free from the <u>law of sin and death</u>.

GOD DOESN'T DO EVIL THAT GOOD MAY COME

CHART # 5

[COVENANT]
[WORD]

GOD
FREE WILL
─SOWING AND REAPING─

LAW OF THE SPIRIT OF LIFE   **LAW OF SIN AND DEATH**

LOVE   *LOVE*   *LOVE*

LOVE   *HATE*

ADAM AND EVE
angels

lucifer

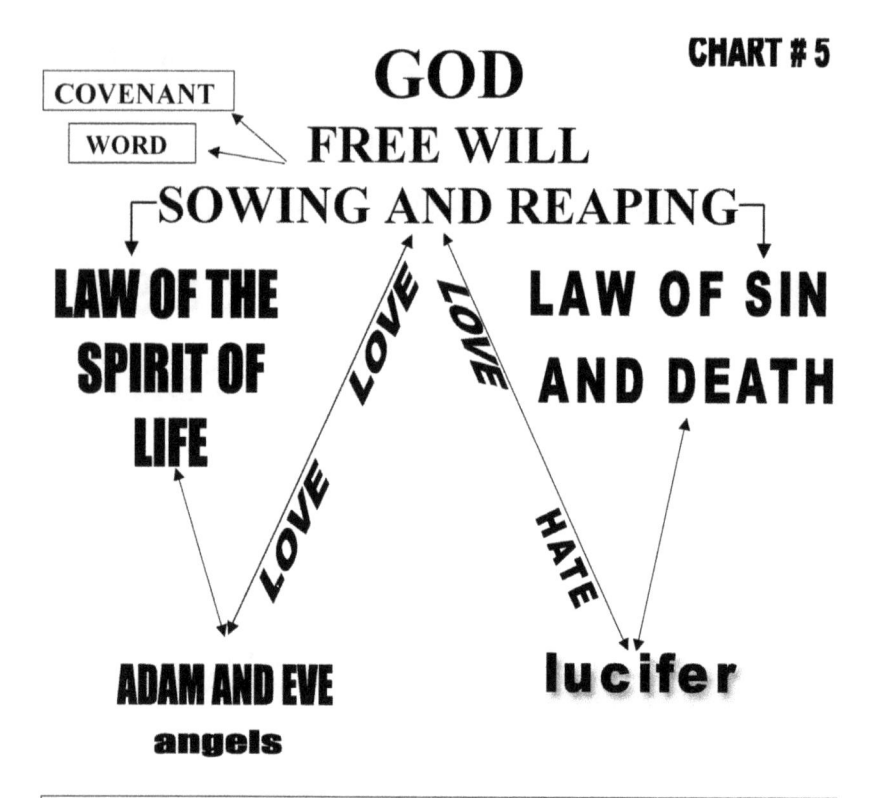

(Gen 1:27 KJV) So God created man in his own image, in the image of God created he him; <u>male and female created he them</u>.
(Gen 5:2 KJV) Male and female created he them; and blessed them, and <u>called their name Adam</u>, in the day when they were created.
(Gen 1:28 KJV) And God <u>blessed them</u>, and God <u>said unto them</u>, Be fruitful, and multiply, and replenish the earth, and <u>subdue it</u>: and have dominion over the fish of the sea, and over the fowl of the air, and over every living thing that moveth upon the earth.
(subdue)= 3533. kabash, kaw-bash'; a prim. root; <u>to tread down</u>; hence neg. to disregard; pos. <u>to conquer</u>, subjugate, violate:--<u>bring into bondage</u>, force<u>, keep under</u>, subdue, <u>bring into subjection.</u>
(Psa 115:16 KJV) The heaven, even the heavens, are the Lord's: but the earth hath he given to the children of men.

CHARTS

CHART # 6

#1 **GOD**
COVENANT
WORD
FREE WILL
#2 ┌─**SOWING AND REAPING**─┐

LAW OF THE SPIRIT OF LIFE   *LOVE*   *LOVE*   **LAW OF SIN AND DEATH**

LOVE   *HATE*

#3 **ADAM AND EVE**   **lucifer**
angels   **FALLEN ANGELS**

God reveals himself in three ways: #1 Deity in heaven, (God the Father) #2 Deity in the covenant, (God the Word) and #3 Deity in Adam and Eve, (God the Holy Spirit)

(John 1:1 KJV) In the beginning was the Word, and the Word was with God, and the Word was God.

GOD DOESN'T DO EVIL THAT GOOD MAY COME

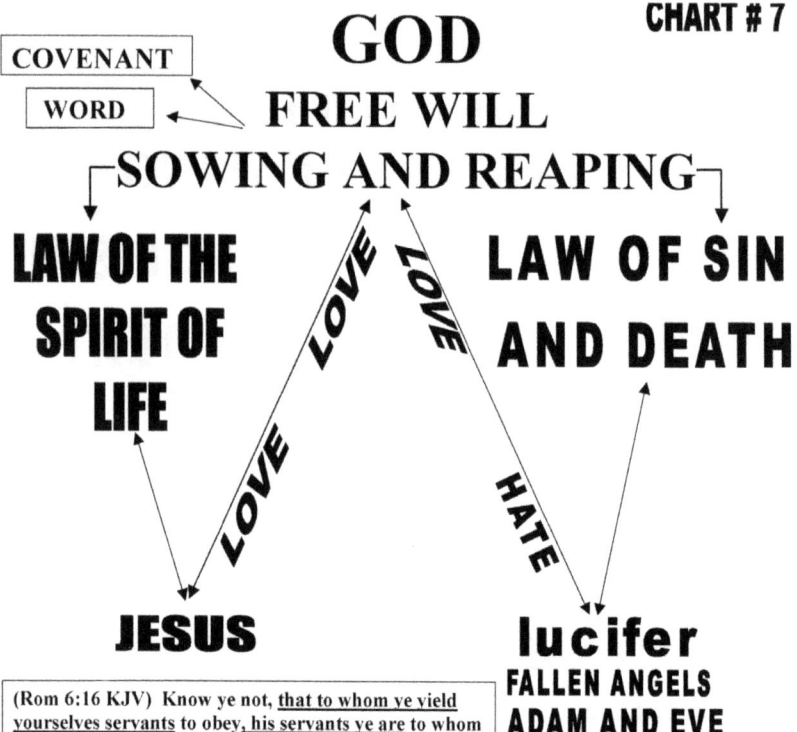

CHART # 7

COVENANT
WORD

GOD
FREE WILL
SOWING AND REAPING

LAW OF THE SPIRIT OF LIFE   **LAW OF SIN AND DEATH**

LOVE   LOVE   LOVE

LOVE   HATE

JESUS   **lucifer**

(Rom 6:16 KJV) Know ye not, that to whom ye yield yourselves servants to obey, his servants ye are to whom ye obey; whether of sin unto death, or of obedience unto righteousness?

FALLEN ANGELS
ADAM AND EVE
ALL MANKIND

(Rom 5:12 KJV) Wherefore, as by one man sin entered into the world, and death by sin; and so death passed upon all men, for that all have sinned:
(Rom 5:17 KJV) For if by one man's offence death reigned by one; much more they which receive abundance of grace and of the gift of righteousness shall reign in life by one, Jesus Christ.)
(Heb 2:14 KJV) Forasmuch then as the children are partakers of flesh and blood, he also himself likewise took part of the same; that through death he might destroy him that had the power of death, that is, the devil;
(Rom 8:1 KJV) There is therefore now no condemnation to them which are in Christ Jesus, who walk not after the flesh, but after the Spirit.
(Rom 8:2 KJV) For the law of the Spirit of life in Christ Jesus hath made me free from the law of sin and death.

CHARTS

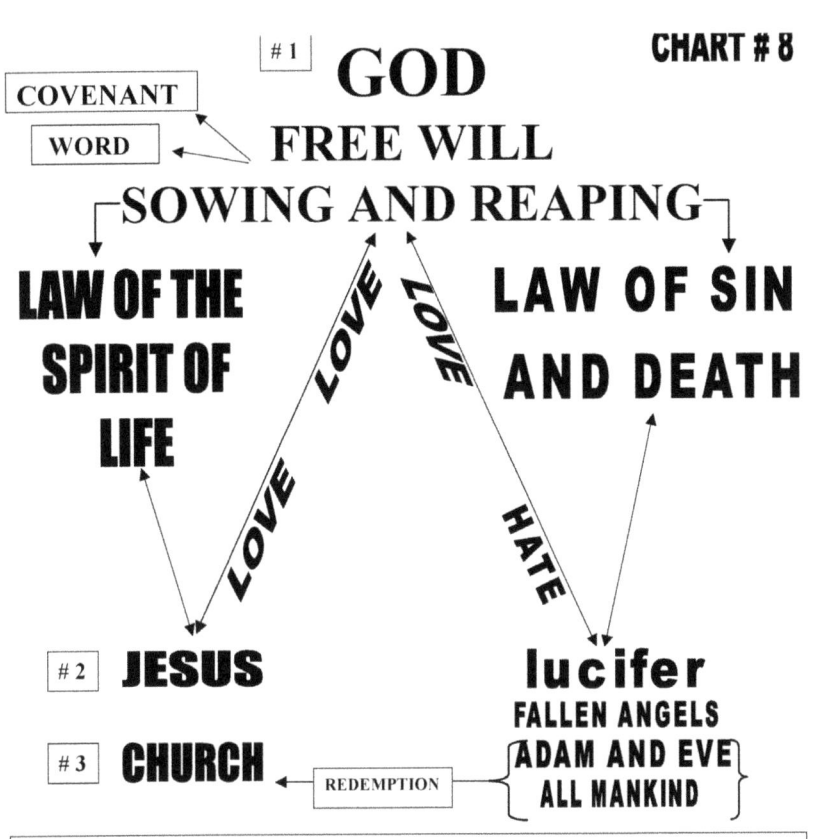

CHART # 8

```
         [COVENANT]        #1  GOD
         [WORD]      ←      FREE WILL
              ┌─── SOWING AND REAPING ───┐
              ↓                           ↓
        LAW OF THE                     LAW OF SIN
        SPIRIT OF      LOVE  LOVE      AND DEATH
          LIFE      LOVE        HATE
              ↓                           ↓
        #2  JESUS                     lucifer
                                      FALLEN ANGELS
        #3  CHURCH  ← REDEMPTION ─    ADAM AND EVE
                                      ALL MANKIND
```

God reveals himself in three ways: #1 Deity in heaven, <u>(God the Father)</u> #2 Deity in Christ, the Word made flesh, <u>(God the Son)</u> and #3 Deity in the Church, <u>(God the Holy Spirit)</u>

(John 1:1 KJV) In the beginning was the <u>Word</u>, and the Word was with God, and the Word was God.(John 1:14 KJV) And the <u>Word was made flesh</u>, and dwelt among us, (and we beheld his glory, the glory as of the only begotten of the Father,) full of grace and truth.
(2 Cor 5:19 KJV) To wit, that <u>God was in Christ</u>, reconciling the world unto himself,
(1 Cor 6:19 KJV) What? know ye not that <u>your body is the temple of the Holy Ghost</u> which is in you, which ye have of God, and ye are not your own?
(Rev 22:17 KJV) And <u>the Spirit and the bride say, Come</u>. And let him that heareth say, Come. And let him that is athirst come. And whosoever will, let him take the water of life freely.

NOTES

CHAPTER 10
The Rest of the Easter Story

1. Charles George Herbermann, et all., *The Catholic Encyclopedia* (New York, The Encyclopedia Press, 1913).

CHAPTER 13
Have We Caused People to Run from God?

1. Lee Strobel, *The Case for Christ:* A Journalist's Personal Investigation of the Evidence for Jesus (Grand Rapids MI: Zonderan, 1998).
2. Ibid.
3. Ibid.
4. Ibid.

CHAPTER 14
Would the Ready God Please Stand Up?

1. Cathy Lynn Grossman and Anthony DeBarros, *USA TODAY*, December 24, 2001, found at http://usatoday30.usatoday.com/life/2001-12-24-religian.htm#more (accessed January 20, 2014).
2. Ibid.

A NOTE FROM THE AUTHOR:

I must tell you where I first heard this revelation of God's Word that includes what we call a missing link in modern theology, being the study of the Law of Sin and Death, which has been called one and the same with God. Changing the character of God that Jesus came and revealed, it took us, the church farther from the authentic truth Jesus taught about the Father. After all Jesus, is the only eyewitness of God the Father. And He spoke and did only what the Father told Him to do and speak.

This revelation of God's character first came to my husband's brother, Keith Porter. It was after many losses in his life that he began a life drawn to prayer and hours of daily Bible study, which has lead into over 30 years of Bible study now. The Holy Spirit quickly showed him that God has never orchestrated the bad situations in anyone's life.

I prayed, "Lord, Is this true? Show me, Lord." It became so real in me that I knew that this message needed to be out to all people! I told Keith, "You need to write books! People need this put in simple language so all people from teens to adults can understand who God is, and the love and help that comes from God."

His answer was, "I can teach it, but I can't write it."

It began burning like fire within me too; I had to let it out! I taught anyone who would listen, especially my clients when there was an open door. And I started feeling like it would be me who would share this awesome revelation of the beautiful character of God in book form.

But I really got my call to write while driving home from work listening to a memorial service at Ground Zero for friends and families after 9/11. It was on live Christian radio, and I started crying so hard and saying loudly: "NO, don't tell them that!" I had to pull off the road in a shopping center parking lot. I thought my heart would break with God's at what God and I had just heard: "Just accept everything that happened here as God's will for everyone that was here."

After crying a while, I heard the Lord speak to me, sounding louder than an audible voice. "Now will you write My book? If it kept one person from taking their life, because they thought I did something bad in their life that I didn't do?"

"Yes, Lord, I will write for You!"

The next week I took off work a few days and started writing with my KJV Bible, the *Strong's Concordance* and a *Webster's Dictionary*. I had no Idea there were three books in the making, and YouTube interviews. God is amazing!

My brother-in-law had moved to another town and his pastor asked him to teach once or twice a week for several

A NOTE FROM THE AUTHOR:

years. Feeling like a lawyer for God, his lessons had at least 100 Bible verses to back each lesson of hope, that God is light, love and there is no darkness in Him at all!

I want to let Keith tell you his story himself about his miracle of God's love by sharing the introduction to his blog:

Keith's Personal Testimony,

Only when I pass a mirror, the reality hits me that sixty-six years have come and gone.

Remembering the storms of life that were harsh at times probably had something to do with the way this stranger in the mirror looks now.

Choices made in how I weathered those storms were based on what I was taught growing up in church. I wish I could say that the church's teachings helped me survive. Unfortunately, it wasn't until I laid aside the teachings of the church and began to search the scriptures for myself that I found the hope and strength to survive.

Dad built churches, pastored, and evangelized for fifty-five years in the Church of God, headquartered in Cleveland TN.

In 1972 I got out of the army, married, and began full time ministry with Dad as an evangelistic team called "The Porter Family." My brother, sister and myself sang as a trio and Dad preached. After about five years, Dad became ill and the ministry as a family evangelistic team ended. I went into construction with my brother.

Church had taught me as a child: 1) that God was in control of everything that happens to us, 2) and that God would not put more on us than what we could bear.

So when life's storms begin to hit me and it was more than I could bear, I was confused, to say the least. Financial loss, mental illness hit my beautiful wife, suicidal depression hit me. Yes, this was more than I could bear. Since the church had taught me that this was all part of God's plan for my life, I became very bitter towards God. It never dawned on me that the church could have been wrong in what they had taught me about God.

They had taught me that God was a God of Wrath; if you did something to displease Him He would take away everything you had and then destroy you. I spent many late night hours trying to figure out what I had done that so displeased God that He would send this terrible storm to destroy me.

I was faithful to attend church, I paid my tithes, I gave to the poor, I was the spiritual head of my house, and I prayed and fasted. I had done everything the church had told me to do.

If this was the way God treated His obedient children, then I didn't want to know this God anymore. If this was

A NOTE FROM THE AUTHOR:

what He had planned for me, it was not worth living. I had planned how I would end my Life and put an end to this misery; put an end to this terrible storm. I felt better thinking, "ust a few more days and it will all be over."

The day before I would end my life in 1992 at age 41 years old, I was sitting next to the window at a restaurant downtown Memphis, TN. Michael and I had gone there for lunch break from a construction job. It was cold that day in late fall; people were walking past the window where I sat with my head resting in my hands, looking out the window thinking, "Tomorrow it will all be over."

But a little old woman walking down the sidewalk in a long winter coat and headscarf stopped right in front of me. She suddenly turned, coming close to the window, and looked at me face to face through the window. Somehow I could hear her through the window as she said: "Don't look so down; it's going to be all right!"

From somewhere deep down inside me where there seemed to be no hope, no light, only darkness, a small glimmer of hope sparked. My sister-in-law Delores called and told me about a revival at a small Assembly of God church not far from where I lived where God was touching people in a special way.

I knew I needed, no, I had to get to that revival. I experienced God's unconditional love in a way I had never known before. There was simply no way the love I felt, the peace I experienced that night came from a God of Wrath, a God that would put me in the hell I had experienced, where it was so dark I no longer wanted to live.

I had to have an answer. Could it be possible that the church I had been raised in, that I had put my trust in, that I had based the way I lived my life on, could the church have been wrong?

I told God I did not believe He had sent the storm that almost took my life. I told Him that I wanted to live and not die, and I meant it. The overwhelming desire for death was gone!

The thought came to me, "Get your Bible and turn to Deuteronomy 30:15 KJV. See, I have set before thee this day Life and Good, and Death and Evil." I said to God, your word says life is good and death is evil. Another thought came to me, yes and God has nothing to do with evil, which is death.

I said, "Well, God, it couldn't have been You that was tempting me to take my life, because that would be evil." Another thought--get your Bible and turn to "James 1:13 KJV. Let no man say when he is tempted, I am tempted of God: for God cannot be tempted with evil, neither tempteth he any man."

I said, "Thank You, God, I'm so glad that it wasn't you that made me feel like I wanted to die."

A NOTE FROM THE AUTHOR:

For the next twenty-five years I took everything the church had taught me and examined it for myself, 1 John 2:27 KJV, "But the Anointing (Holy Spirit) which ye have received of him abideth in you, and Ye Need Not That Any Man Teach You: but as the same Anointing (Holy Spirit) teacheth you of all things, and is truth, and is no lie, and even as it hath taught you, ye shall abide in him."

Read and examine what others teach, but your final authority in what you believe is based on what you and your own personal Rabbi (the Holy Spirit in you) agree on.

This blog, along with the YouTube videos, are some of the answers I believe God has given me to the questions I have had.

1 Peter 3:15 KJV, "But sanctify the Lord God in your hearts: and be ready always to give an answer to every man that asketh you a reason of the hope that is in you with meekness and fear."

By Keith Porter

Keith's teaching lessons were taped and are now available on YouTube with Scriptures and graphs on most of them for easier understanding. Here are a couple of the titles:

"Keith Porter: In the Beginning"

"Keith Porter: End Time Events"

Contact Author Information:
delores@truthandhopeministries.com
or
Delores J. Porter
P.O. Box 722
Hernando, MS 38632